1745
AND ALL THAT
The Story of the Highlands
SCOULAR ANDERSON

For Matt

1745
AND ALL THAT
The Story of the Highlands
SCOULAR ANDERSON

BIRLINN

First published in Great Britain in 2001 by
Birlinn Limited
West Newington House
10 Newington Road
Edinburgh EH9 1QS

www.birlinn.co.uk

Reprinted 2005, 2011

ISBN13: 978 1 84158 129 3

British Library Cataloguing-in-Publication Data
A Catalogue record for this book is available from
the British Library

Printed and bound by CPI Antony Rowe, Chippenham, Wiltshire

CONTENTS

The Early Times

This is the story of the Highlands of Scotland. The bit that's called the Highlands is not all high. Some of it is quite low, and a lot of it is made up of islands.

THE BOUNDARY IS VERY VAGUE BUT *THE HIGHLANDS* USUALLY MEANS THE NORTH-WEST HALF OF SCOTLAND.

OUTER HEBRIDES

INNER HEBRIDES

ATLANTIC OCEAN

SHETLAND

ORKNEY

INVERNESS

HIGHLANDS

NORTH SEA

GLASGOW

EDINBURGH

LOWLANDS

The story starts about 10,000 years ago. Scotland was not called Scotland, and the Highlands were just a bunch of high mountains, soggy bogs and water. Lots of water – mist, rain, streams, rivers, lochans, lochs and wide stretches of wild sea.

Then into this landscape came something that had never been seen before – humans. They came up from the south, moving slowly along the coast, most probably by boat.

These were stone-age people, and if they could have sent a postcard, it would have looked something like this:

Dear Family Flatnose,
– BIG forests and BIG animals!
Lots of bog and lots of
mountains – makes
travelling a teensy bit
tricky. However, plenty of
water so we've been
sightseeing by boat.
Very peaceful, no crowds –
we might stay a while.
Wish you were here!
Yours, Family Bigfeet

Family Flatnose
Home Camp
The knoll
By the River
        Narrows

These stone-age people moved around a lot. Home camp got a bit grotty and smelly after a while, and all the nearby firewood got used up. Their travels might have been something like this:

BIG FEET FAMILY AND FLATNOSE FAMILY
PROGRAMME OF EVENTS

EVENT ONE
(LEAVE RIVER CAMP AND GO TO SEASIDE CAMP)

CATCH FISH. DRY AND SMOKE FISH FOR LATER USE.
UGO AND EBBI GO TO ISLAND-OF-STONES TO LOOK FOR GOOD STONES FOR MAKING TOOLS.

EVENT TWO
(MOVE TO WOOD CAMP)

COLLECT BERRIES AND NUTS. FISH IN RIVER.
MOBBO AND UMBI TO THE HILL CAMP TO CATCH DEER FOR BIG FEAST. AND MAYBE A BEAR FUR TO MAKE A HAT FOR GUMBA - BIG, PLEASE.

EVENT THREE
(TO THE BIG CAVE)

ANIMAL SKINS TO BE PREPARED FOR CLOTHES. MAKE CLOTHES. MAKE TOOLS. WEAVE HEATHER INTO ROPES. MAKE CONTAINERS OUT OF BARK
DEAD BUSY. THEN BIG PARTY.

EVENT FOUR

MOVE BACK TO RIVER CAMP WHEN WEATHER IMPROVES. COLLECT STUFF FOR TENTS.

These people have left us a few clues about their lifestyle. On some of the islands there are huge middens – piles of seashells left over from countless fishy suppers.

Sometimes, lots of shards of sharp stones are found. This means that this was a place where stones were 'knapped' – chipped into sharp tools. No stone-age man or woman went without a good tool-kit.

Life was hard work but now and again there was time to have some friends round and enjoy a ceilidh.

The Time of the Axe

FROM ABOUT 4,000 BC

After a couple of thousand years, people with new ideas began to arrive in the west.

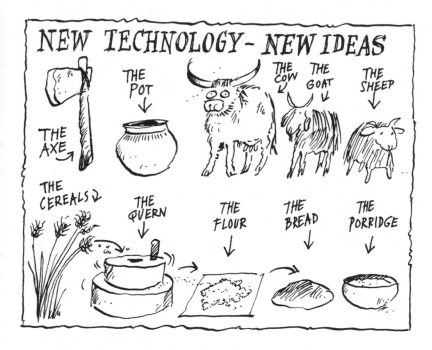

NEW TECHNOLOGY - NEW IDEAS

THE AXE

THE POT

THE COW

THE GOAT

THE SHEEP

THE CEREALS

THE QUERN

THE FLOUR

THE BREAD

THE PORRIDGE

These people were farmers. They wanted to settle down in one place, build a house, grow their crops and tend their animals.

This meant the trees had to go.

After a while, it was time to improve the technology. The stone axe was replaced by the bronze axe, then the bronze axe was upgraded to the iron axe.

The farmers were also improving the look of their houses. There were all sorts of designs.

On the wild and windy west coasts, or on the islands, you might prefer something substantial in stone.

In the glens, a wooden house was more comfortable.

As time went by, people began to get grand ideas. Or perhaps they were feeling a little insecure. A fortified house would certainly make your neighbours think twice about coming to bother you. Fortified houses were a bit like castles – designed to keep enemies out.

IN THE NORTH, PEOPLE BUILT TOWERS OF STONE CALLED BROCHS.

IN THE SOUTH, DUNS WERE MORE COMMON. A HOUSE OR HOUSES WERE BUILT ON A HIGH PLACE, SURROUNDED BY DITCHES AND A WALL OR FENCE. CRANNOGS WERE HOUSES BUILT ON ISLANDS ON LOCHS.

These people also built houses for their dead. Like the houses for the living, they came in many shapes and sizes. There were small ones, grand ones, and ones that had room for lots of bodies.

BURIAL CAIRN NEAR INVERNESS. IT WOULD HAVE BEEN COVERED OVER WITH STONES AND EARTH.

When they were feeling really energetic, people got very creative with stones. They sculpted cup-and-ring patterns on small rocks. They pushed big rocks into circles.

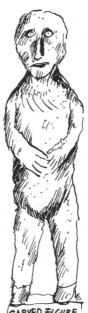

The stone circles may have had something to do with the people's religion.

They also threw valuable items – wooden dishes, spear-heads etc. – into lochs and rivers as gifts to their gods.

CARVED FIGURE FROM LOCHABER. PERHAPS A GODDESS OR SPIRIT THE PEOPLE WORSHIPPED.

In the next chapter: the Romans have pushed off, the King puts his foot in it, and the magic marker makes the Memory Master morose.

MEANWHILE... *in the other part of* Scotland... THE ROMANS HAD ARRIVED...

THEY DIDN'T MUCH FANCY MARCHING DEEP INTO THE HIGHLAND GLENS BUT THEIR SHIPS PASSED THROUGH THE ISLANDS, SPYING.

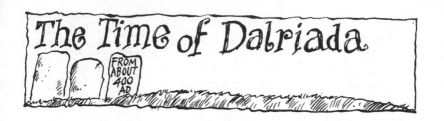

The Time of Dalriada

FROM ABOUT 400 AD

The maze of mountains made it a bit difficult for people in the west to communicate with the rest of Scotland. But that didn't bother them much, because the seas and lochs of the west were a bit like a motorway which they could use to visit friends and relatives nearby and do a bit of trading, too.

Sometimes, visitors just took over. People from the kingdom of Dalriada in Ireland moved across to the nearest part of Scotland and made themselves comfortable. To feel at home, they gave their new territory the same name.

THE PEOPLE FROM IRELAND WERE CALLED *SCOTTI* BY THE ROMANS. THE *SCOTTI* CALLED THEMSELVES GAELS. EVENTUALLY, *DALRIADA* TOOK ON A NEW NAME — *OIRER GAIDHEAL* — MEANING *THE COAST OF THE GAELS*. THIS NAME CHANGED ITS SPELLING OVER CENTURIES TO BECOME ARGYLL.

DAL RIADA

DUNADD

DALRIADA

Eventually, the Dalriada in Scotland was divided up between family groups, known as Cenela (kindred) or Clann (children).

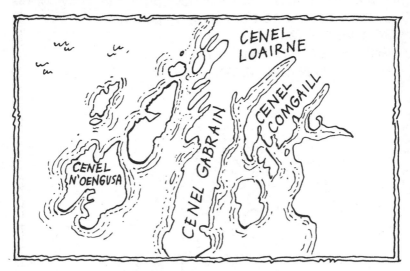

However, there were problems.

LIST of TROUBLE SPOTS
1. TOO MANY KINGS
2. BIG FAMILIES- BIG TROUBLE

When it was time to choose a leader it was done at a family conference. However, though everyone in the clan was equal, some were a little bit more equal than others. The king or chief was usually chosen from the posh branch of the family.

Sometimes, there was family bickering, with different branches of the family choosing their own leader.

THINGS TO DO ONCE YOU BECOME MOST IMPORTANT KING of DALRIADA

1 Go to Dunadd, the chief fort of Dalriada.

2 Be sworn in as chief or king at a special ceremony. (You could be kicked out again if you didn't come up to expectations.)

PLACE FOOT IN FOOT-SHAPED HOLLOW IN ROCK SYMBOLIZING MARRIAGE WITH THE LAND.

BARD RECITING A FLATTERING POEM.

PRIESTS DOING ALL SORTS OF FANCY THINGS.

3 Have a big party. Drink wine from glass goblets imported from France and eat exotic sweetmeats like dates. (They knew how to do things in style.)

4 Travel round your land making your presence felt. Give gifts (like a jewelled brooch), receive gifts (like a cow). Everyone's happy.

5 Promise to protect your people, but make sure you have the right number of warriors to man the ships of your navy.

Each group of 20 houses must supply 28 fit, warrior oarsmen.

That is, enough men to crew 2 ships with 7 benches each side.

The ships should be the usual type- wicker framework covered in skins.

I, the King's Memory Master, have spoken!

The king's records of who did what, who owned what and who owed what were kept in the head of the *filidh* – the king's Memory Master. But a new technology arrived to make things easier – writing. So a census was drawn up, listing all the inhabitants in the land and their property.

In the next chapter, King Brude might buy the Book, preachers pick peaceful places, carvers get curly with crosses.

MEANWHILE...
in the other part of Scotland...
THE REST OF SCOTLAND WAS DIVIDED UP BETWEEN ANGLES, BRITONS AND PICTS.

SOME PICTS

PICTS

DAL RIADA

ANGLES

BRITONS

THE PICTS LIVED MOSTLY IN THE NORTH-EAST, BUT SOME LIVED ON THE WEST COAST AND ON THE ISLANDS.

Among the people who came to Dalriada, one group were different from the rest. They wore strange clothes, cut their hair in a strange way and carried a bag which contained strange things – books and writing materials.

Read any good books lately?

They were Christian monks, and they brought a new religion to Scotland. They made their way up the west coast and settled on many of the islands. Sometimes they just built a hut, but sometimes they built monasteries.

The islands suited them just fine:

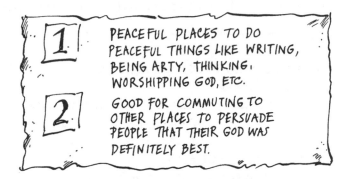

1 PEACEFUL PLACES TO DO PEACEFUL THINGS LIKE WRITING, BEING ARTY, THINKING, WORSHIPPING GOD, ETC.

2 GOOD FOR COMMUTING TO OTHER PLACES TO PERSUADE PEOPLE THAT THEIR GOD WAS DEFINITELY BEST.

ISLAND MONASTERY COMPLEX

MONKS' QUARTERS

HOSTEL FOR VISITORS

MEETING ROOM

CHURCH

WRITING ROOM and LIBRARY

REFECTORY (DINING-ROOM) AND KITCHEN

WORKSHOPS

Iona was one of the islands the monks chose to settle on.
It became famous when a man called Columba arrived.

PERSONAL FILE : COLUMBA
COLUMBA (MEANING DOVE) NOT REAL NAME
BIRTHPLACE : IRELAND
REASON FOR VISITING :   INVOLVED IN A LITTLE ARGUMENT
                         (WITH SWORDS) BACK HOME – BEST
                         TO LIE LOW FOR A BIT.
OCCUPATION : CHRISTIAN MONK
QUALITIES :   ENERGETIC, GETS THINGS DONE.
SPECIALITIES : LIKES TRAVELLING, READING, WRITING.
AIMS :   TO CONVERT PEOPLE TO THE CHRISTIAN
               RELIGION.
IN HIS SIGHTS : KING BRUDE OF THE PICTS.

Columba travelled up the Great Glen to the court of
King Brude at Inverness. It was a mission of mixed
success and Columba didn't manage to convert everyone.
You win some, you lose some.

30

Eventually, the island of Iona became the Christian headquarters of Dalriada and the burial place of many kings.

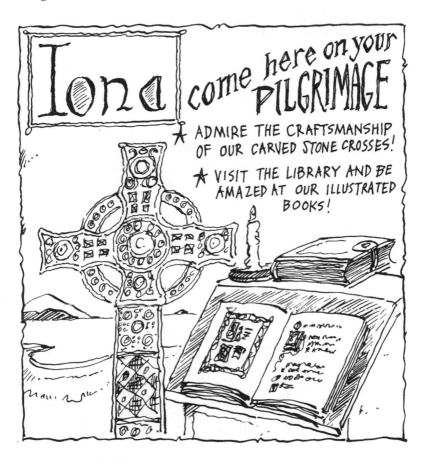

In the next chapter, Sigurd seeks a stretch southwards, seafarers snatch silver and slaves, Vikings carve up the country.

The Time of Vikings

FROM ABOUT 800

They came from Norway in fast ships and with a fiendish gleam in their eyes. The Vikings were here. At first, they seemed nasty pieces of work (but probably no worse than other people in those days). Then they settled down, built houses and became buddies with the locals.

The Vikings were expert shipbuilders. They sailed their
ships as far away as Russia and Turkey in the east, and
America in the west. Compared to that, Scotland
was in their own back yard.

The Vikings used their fast longships to explore and pillage. (Pillaging means raiding.)

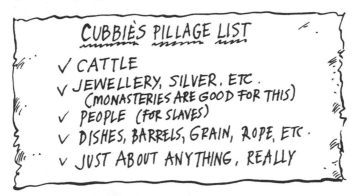

CUBBIE'S PILLAGE LIST

✓ CATTLE
✓ JEWELLERY, SILVER, ETC.
   (MONASTERIES ARE GOOD FOR THIS)
✓ PEOPLE (FOR SLAVES)
✓ DISHES, BARRELS, GRAIN, ROPE, ETC.
✓ JUST ABOUT ANYTHING, REALLY

But back home in Norway, it was becoming a bit of a squash. There were too many people and good farmland was becoming scarce. Many Vikings decided to pull out the *Knarr* (cargo boat), fill it with everything but the kitchen sink and look for some nice little place abroad to settle down.

SHETLAND WAS ONLY A DAY'S SAIL FROM NORWAY. ORKNEY HAD GOOD SOIL. THE VIKINGS TOOK THEM OVER. THE NORWEGIAN KING GAVE THE ISLANDS TO SIGURD THE MIGHTY WHO BECAME FIRST EARL OF ORKNEY. FROM THERE THE VIKINGS MOVED DOWN THE WEST COAST. THE EARLDOM OF ORKNEY BEGAN TO STRETCH FURTHER AND FURTHER.

SHETLAND

NORWAY

ORKNEY

VIKING BITS

The Vikings built their farmhouses on the islands. They were long buildings of stone with turf roofs.

They may have been wild warriors, but the Vikings had a soft spot for beautiful things. They had fidgety fingers – anything that didn't move was decorated. Give a Viking a piece of wood (or stone, or bone) and he or she would carve something on it.

ANIMALS SHARED THE HOUSE

BENCHES FOR SITTING OR SLEEPING ON

THE VIKINGS WERE ADVENTUROUS TRADERS. THEY TRAVELLED FAR AND WIDE ACROSS EUROPE, SELLING AND EXCHANGING GOODS.

COOKING POT SUSPENDED FROM BEAM ←

← WOMAN WEAVING

What Vikings liked best of all was silver, and they collected it eagerly.

SILVER ITEMS

SILVER RING MONEY

EASIEST WAY TO CARRY DOSH

HACK SILVER—SILVER ITEMS CUT INTO BITS OF EQUAL WEIGHT TO USE AS COINS

Sometimes, in a tricky situation, they buried their collection. Sometimes the owner never came back for it. He might have been killed or simply forgotten where it was. Viking silver hoards are still discovered to this day.

I'M sure it's thirty-nine paces from the tree beside the round stone to the left of the rock that looks like a rabbit.

The Vikings were pagans. They had many gods, such as Odin, who rode a horse with eight legs and had a bodyguard of women called Valkyries. Frigg was the goddess of health and happiness. Thor was the god of thunder.

PEOPLE WORE REPLICAS OF THOR'S HAMMER (HE THUMPED IT AGAINST THE SKY TO MAKE THUNDER) AS A GOOD LUCK CHARM. WHEN THEY BECAME CHRISTIANS THEY WORE A CROSS — AND SOMETIMES THE HAMMER, TOO, JUST TO BE ON THE SAFE SIDE.

THOR'S HAMMER

CHRISTIAN CROSS

When Vikings died, they hoped they would go to join their gods in the heavenly kingdom of Valhalla. Some of their possessions were usually put into their graves.

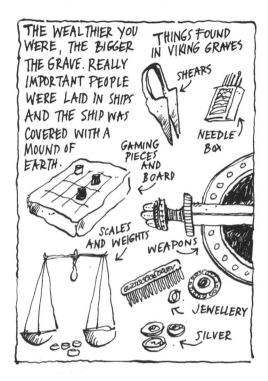

THE WEALTHIER YOU WERE, THE BIGGER THE GRAVE. REALLY IMPORTANT PEOPLE WERE LAID IN SHIPS AND THE SHIP WAS COVERED WITH A MOUND OF EARTH.

THINGS FOUND IN VIKING GRAVES

SHEARS

NEEDLE BOX

GAMING PIECES AND BOARD

SCALES AND WEIGHTS

WEAPONS

JEWELLERY

SILVER

In the next chapter, Vikings vanquished by marine modification, the Lordships live it up on the loch, the Lordships find themselves in deep water.

MEANWHILE... in the other part of Scotland...

THE SCOTS AND PICTS HAD PEACEFULLY JOINED THEIR KINGDOMS TOGETHER. KENNETH M°ALPIN OF DALRIADA BECAME THE FIRST KING OF SCOTS.

These Vikings are a pain in the neck!

Pack the bags!

BECAUSE OF VIKING TROUBLE, KEN MOVED HIS HEADQUARTERS FURTHER EAST ACROSS SCOTLAND. LATER, THE SCOTS TOOK OVER THE KINGDOMS OF THE BRITONS AND ANGLES IN THE SOUTH.

The Time of Ships

FROM ABOUT 1100

There were now two languages used in the west of Scotland. The Vikings spoke Norse and the Gaels spoke Gaelic. This could be confusing.

Things sorted themselves out because the Vikings began to speak Gaelic. It was also becoming difficult to tell a Gael from a Viking. Some people called the Vikings Gael-Galls – Foreign Gaels.

PLACE NAMES IN THE WEST WERE NOW
A BIT OF A MIXTURE - SOME VIKING,
SOME GAELIC, SOME A COMBINATION OF
BOTH

MOST
NAMES ON
ORKNEY AND
SHETLAND ARE
NORSE

IN THE OUTER
ISLES, NORSE FJELL
(MOUNTAIN) BECAME
VAL
E.G. Heaval
Ronneval

A NORSE WORD MEANING
TURNING POINT (BECAUSE
VIKING SHIPS TURNED
HERE TO SAIL SOUTH)
GAVE THIS CAPE ITS
NAME - WRATH

NORSE EY
(ISLAND)BECAME
AY
E.G. PABBAY
ERISKAY
ROTHESAY
ISLAY

STAC POLLY
NORSE - STAC (MOUNTAIN)
AND
GAELIC - POLLAIDH (POOL)

NORSE - VIK
(BAY) BECAME WICK
E.G. WICK
LERWICK
BUT THE GAELS
CHANGED IT TO
AIG
E.G. MALLAIG
ARISAIG

ARDTORNISH
GAELIC- ARD (HEADLAND)
AND
NORSE - THORI (A MAN'S NAME)
AND
NORSE - NESS (HEADLAND)
AGAIN!

NAMES ENDING IN
BOL
BISTER
BUSTER
BOST
BUS
(NORSE - FARM OR
STEADING) ARE
FOUND THROUGHOUT THE ISLANDS

But just who was in charge of the Highlands? A rattle of a spear at your gate could mean the heavies of Harald Fairhair had come to say hello. Or maybe they were the men of Olav the Red, or Diarmad MacMaelnambo or Bjorn Cripplehand or, worst of all, the unpleasant Viking, Godred of Man.

There were an awful lot of little kings wanting to be big kings and it could be uncomfortable if you got in their way.

One of these kings made more of a mark on history than the others. He was Somerled, King of Argyll. He decided that Godred needed taking down a peg or two. He had a plan.

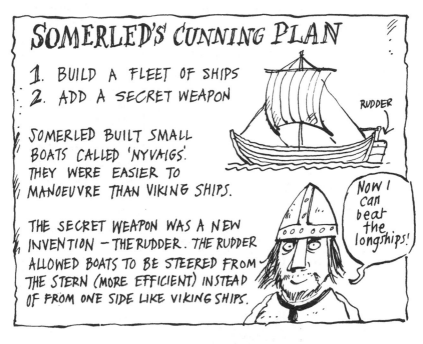

In a sea-battle off the coast of the island of Islay, Somerled defeated the Vikings. This was a terrible shock to them.

Somerled's territory now stretched the length of the west coast of Scotland. But remember, there was always a bigger king somewhere ready to make you feel uncomfortable. The King of Norway, leader of the Vikings, still saw himself as Top Dog in the west of Scotland.

MEANWHILE...
In the other part of Scotland...
KING MALCOLM IV OF SCOTLAND WAS DISHING OUT LAND TO HIS PALS – ANGLO-NORMAN NOBLES WHO HAD COME UP FROM ENGLAND.
(THEY WERE THE DESCENDANTS OF THE NORMANS WHO HAD INVADED ENGLAND IN 1066.)
(THEY IN TURN WERE DESCENDANTS OF VIKINGS. VERY CONFUSING.)
You can have all these lands – but keep the locals under control-eh?
Say no more, Sire!

Also, the favourites of the King of Scotland were setting up home closer and closer to Somerled's territory. He decided it was time to act.

Somerled got together a large fleet and sailed up the Firth of Clyde to Renfrew. He was going to show King Malcolm just how much muscle he had.

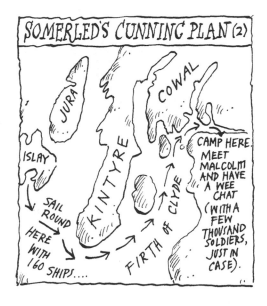

SOMERLED'S CUNNING PLAN (2)

JURA

COWAL

ISLAY

KINTYRE

FIRTH OF CLYDE

SAIL ROUND HERE WITH 160 SHIPS....

CAMP HERE. MEET MALCOLM AND HAVE A WEE CHAT (WITH A FEW THOUSAND SOLDIERS, JUST IN CASE).

Unfortunately, Somerled was found dead in his tent (perhaps murdered). The men of the west retreated with the body of their great leader.

The Kingdom of the Isles was now handed down from father to son. Sometimes the Kings of Scotland and the Isles were on speaking terms, more often not. King Angus Mor (Big Angus) I was sitting in his Islay stronghold one day when he received a communication from King Hakon of Norway.

But the Scottish king got wind of this and acted quickly . . .

Angus pointed out to Hakon that he was now in a very delicate position. Hakon replied . . .

Angus reluctantly agreed to join Hakon.

But at the Battle of Largs the Vikings were thoroughly defeated.

It was the end of Viking influence in the west of Scotland.

Angus II of the Isles became great pals with King Robert the Bruce of Scotland. He took a company of fighting men to help him out at the Battle of Bannockburn. The two leaders sometimes met up for a jar or two of ale.

By the time of John I (Lord of the Isles, as he now called himself), the HQ of the Kingdom of the Isles was at Finlaggan, an island in the middle of a loch in the middle of the island of Islay.

You could take a boat to the island or walk along a causeway. Another causeway led to the Council Island where John had business meetings with his chiefs.

FOR CENTURIES THE KINGS OF THE ISLES USED THE GREAT SEAL OF ISLAY ON ALL THEIR OFFICIAL DOCUMENTS. AN ANCIENT CELTIC LEGEND SAID THAT IF YOUR ENEMY PUT NINE WAVES BETWEEN HIS SHIP AND YOURS, YOU WOULD NEVER CATCH HIM. THE SEAL SHOWS THE LITTLE SHIP OF SOMERLED PLOUGHING THROUGH NINE WAVES AND THEREFORE VANQUISHING THE ENEMY.

FERRY

CHURCH

If there had been celeb magazines in those times, this is what they might have contained . . .

LORD OF THE ISLES WELCOMES IMPORTANT GUESTS TO HIS LUXURY HOME AT FINLAGGAN ON ISLAY

FINLAGGAN MUSICIANS GET FEET TAPPING AT LORDSHIP'S FEASTS

ANGUS OF KEILLS SHOWS OFF HIS ROMAN PILGRIM'S BADGE. 'THE TRIP TO ROME WAS THE HIGHLIGHT OF MY LIFE!' HE CLAIMS.

THE LADY OF LAGGAN SUPERVISES THE SERVICE OF WINE TO HER GUESTS

HEAD COOK PULLS OUT ALL STOPS TO PROVIDE MOUTHWATERING FEAST

MEANWHILE...
in the other
part of
Scotland...

KING ROBERT III
WAS SICKLY AND
HOPELESS. HIS SON,
JAMES I, BEGAN
HIS KINGSHIP IN
CAPTIVITY IN
ENGLAND SO HIS UNCLE,
DUKE OF ALBANY, RAN
THE COUNTRY.

I'm in
charge.

THE FIRST FOUR
KING JAMESES CAME
TO STICKY ENDS—
TWO WERE MURDERED,
ONE WAS BLOWN UP
BY A CANNON AND
ONE WAS KILLED IN
BATTLE.

Donald II, Lord of the Isles, decided to throw his weight about. He claimed that a large chunk (1) of Scotland was really his. He raised an army and marched towards Aberdeen.

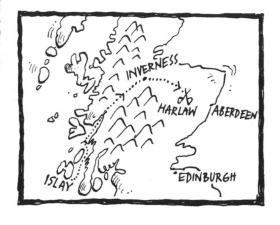

The Duke of Albany (2) sent an army led by the Earl of Mar (3) to meet Donald.(4) The two armies met at Harlaw and slugged it out.(5) So much blood was shed that the event became known as Red Harlaw. Donald achieved nothing and went back home.

52

HANDY NOTES

① THIS WAS THE EARLDOM OF ROSS WHICH THE LORD OF THE ISLES' WIFE HAD INHERITED.

② ALBANY REALLY WANTED THE EARLDOM OF ROSS FOR HIS OWN SON. ALBANY, BY THE WAY, HAD KILLED HIS NEPHEW (KING ROBERT III's SON) BY LOCKING HIM IN A TOWER AND FORGETTING TO FEED HIM.

③ THE EARL OF MAR WASN'T MUCH NICER — REGARDED AS A RUTHLESS GANG-LEADER. HIS FATHER, EARL OF BUCHAN, GAINED THE NICKNAME 'WOLF OF BADENOCH' FOR HIS UNPLEASANT HABITS WHICH INCLUDED STEALING TREASURE FROM ELGIN CATHEDRAL THEN BURNING THE TOWN TO THE GROUND.

④ THIS WAS VERY MUCH A FAMILY QUARREL AS DONALD OF THE ISLES WAS ACTUALLY KING JAMES I· OF SCOTLAND'S COUSIN.

⑤ SLUGGING IT OUT WAS A COMMON PASTIME. ABOUT THIS TIME, A WOODEN ENCLOSURE WAS BUILT AT PERTH SO THAT TWO CLANS COULD SETTLE AN ARGUMENT BY ARMED COMBAT. THEY WERE ALLOWED 30 MEN EACH. (ONE CLAN WAS A MAN SHORT SO A LOCAL BLACKSMITH WAS CALLED IN TO MAKE UP THE NUMBERS.) NOT MANY SURVIVED. THE KING CAME TO WATCH THE MATCH.

LET'S FACE IT, IN THESE TIMES YOU WOULDN'T EVEN TRUST YOUR GRANNY.

In the time of John II of the Isles, fortunes began to go downhill for the Lords of the Isles. John made the mistake of teaming up with the wrong people.

BAD COMPANY 1   THE EARL OF DOUGLAS (THE DOUGLAS FAMILY WERE ARCH-ENEMIES OF THE KINGS OF SCOTLAND).

BAD COMPANY 2   KING EDWARD IV OF ENGLAND (THE KINGS OF ENGLAND WERE ALWAYS ENEMIES OF SCOTLAND).

They hatched a plot.

A CUNNING PLAN (PRIVATE AND CONFIDENTIAL)
1 ~ GET RID OF KING OF SCOTLAND
THEN...
2 ~ LORD OF THE ISLES CAN BE IN CHARGE OF THE WHOLE OF THE NORTH BIT OF SCOTLAND
3 ~ EARL OF DOUGLAS CAN BE IN CHARGE OF THE SOUTH.
4 ~ KING OF ENGLAND CAN BE BOSS OVER THE WHOLE LOT

King James III was tipped off about this.

I thought this intercepted letter might interest you, Sire.

James III was furious. He had tolerated the Lord of the Isles because he kept things under control in the west, but now he was seriously stepping out of line. King James told John just what was what.

Dear Sir,
I will not put up with treasonable behaviour! Your title, lands and rights are forfeit (i.e. they are now mine). Any arguments and I'll send in the military.
Yours, James (King).

John agreed to behave but his son, Angus, did not. Like a spoilt child, he went on the rampage, burning a few towns. Father and son eventually fought it out in a sea-battle off the coast of the island of Mull. Angus won but was murdered shortly after.

The new King of Scotland, James IV, had the Lord of the Isles brought to Edinburgh in chains and put on trial. The end of the Lords of the Isles had come.

In the next chapter, bards get boastful over clan claims, monarchs get mad over challenging chiefs, confusing choices put skulls on spikes.

The Time of Chiefs

FROM ABOUT 1400

The chief's bard steps towards the firelight. It is his job to retell the history of the clan and its daring exploits.

... and Fergus Mor lifted the huge rock from the flank of Ben Trivet and killed twenty men with one blow...

During feasting and drinking in the chief's hall, members of the clan liked to hear these things, and the more fanciful the better. It made them feel good and together. It was like watching a video.

But clanship was a very hazy thing. Who belonged to which clan? Clans suddenly appeared or died out. Relatives of chiefs started clans of their own. Clan lands were lost and gained. Some clan members lived on lands that belonged to another clan which was their bitter enemy.

The chief of the clan was responsible for those living on his land. He was in charge of their welfare and they looked to him for guidance. He led them into battle if necessary.

THE CHIEF

THE CHIEF'S HENCHMAN— BODYGUARD AND SERVANT WHO LISTENED IN ON ALL CONVERSATIONS TO MAKE SURE NO ONE WAS INSULTING HIS CHIEF.

GILLE-AIRM — CHIEF'S ARMOUR-BEARER

GILLE-CAS-FLIUCH — CARRIED CHIEF THROUGH STREAMS OR TO AND FROM BOATS

The top chiefs liked to put on a show when travelling or visiting. They took many people with them. They were known as the chief's 'tail' and the more important the chief, the bigger the tail. The chief's attendants might include . . .

THE CHIEF'S PIPER – REGARDED AS A GENTLEMAN AND THEREFORE DID NOT CARRY HIS OWN PIPES

CHIEF'S MESSENGER

GILLE-PIOBAIR – THE PIPER'S SERVANT

GILLE-TRUIS-AIRNIS – CHIEF'S BAGGAGE-MAN

MOST PEOPLE WORE THE PLAID. IF YOU WANTED A
GARMENT SUITABLE FOR THE WEST OF SCOTLAND THEN
THIS WAS IT. IT ALLOWED EASY MOVEMENT OVER
ROUGH TERRAIN AS WELL AS BEING WARM AND
WINDPROOF. RAIN MADE THE FIBRES OF THE WOOLLEN
PLAID SWELL TO PRODUCE A WATERPROOF COVERING.

PUTTING ON THE PLAID (GAELIC- BREACAN OR FEILEADH-BHREACAIN - THE BELTED PLAID).

① LAY BELT ON
GROUND

② LAY PLAID ON
BELT

③ FOLD BOTTOM PART
TO YOUR TASTE

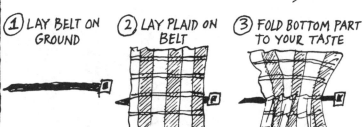

④ LIE DOWN ON
PLAID AND
FASTEN BELT
ROUND WAIST

TOP PART OF PLAID COULD BE WORN OVER
SHOULDERS OR HEAD, FASTENED ON LEFT
SHOULDER (KEEPING SWORD-ARM FREE) OR
LOOPED AT SIDES (HANDY FOR CARRYING
THINGS).

PEOPLE USUALLY WENT BAREFOOT IN SUMMER OR WORE SOCKS AND LEATHER SHOES.

THERE WAS NO SUCH THING AS CLAN TARTAN, THOUGH EACH DISTRICT PROBABLY HAD ITS OWN SPECIAL PATTERN.

GARTER OF STRAW

LOCAL PLANTS SUPPLIED DYES OF SUBTLE HUES – BROWNS, GREENS AND YELLOWS.

BROG – VERY LIGHT LEATHER – GOOD FOR RUNNING IN

A SPRIG OF A CERTAIN PLANT SHOWED WHICH FAMILY YOU BELONGED TO – PINNED TO CLOTHES OR HAT – THOUGH MOST HIGHLANDERS WENT WITHOUT HATS AND WORE THEIR HAIR LONG.

IN BATTLE, CLANSMEN SOMETIMES THREW OFF THEIR PLAIDS AND FOUGHT WITH THEIR LONG SHIRTS TIED BETWEEN THEIR LEGS

EEE AGH!

HIGHLAND GENTLEMEN WORE TRIUBHAS (TREWS) – TIGHT-FITTING TO REDUCE CHAFING.

WOMEN WORE THE EARASAID – A VERSION OF THE PLAID.

ONLY TOP PEOPLE HAD A SPORAN – LEATHER PURSES OF BADGER OR GOAT SKIN.

THE MOST IMPORTANT CHIEFS LIVED IN CASTLES — USUALLY NEAR WATER AS A BOAT WAS STILL THE BEST WAY TO TRAVEL — NO ROADS.

PLOUGHS WERE PULLED BY GARRONS (SMALL PONIES) BUT THE CAS CHROM (FOOT PLOUGH) WAS BETTER FOR ROUGH OR STEEP GROUND.

LARGE HERDS OF CATTLE WERE BRED FOR EXPORT TO THE LOWLANDS. IN SUMMER, THE CATTLE (+ SHEEP AND GOATS) WERE TAKEN TO SHIELINGS — SUMMER PASTURES UP IN THE HILLS.

GROUND CULTIVATED IN STRIPS OF OATS AND BARLEY ALSO FLAX TO MAKE LINEN CLOTH

CLANSPEOPLE LIVED IN HOUSES WITH TURF WALLS, THATCHED WITH STRAW OR HEATHER HELD DOWN BY STONES.

PEAT FOR FUEL ON FIRE

HIGHLAND MENU
CHICKEN
FISH
MILK, CREAM, BUTTER, CHEESE
PORRIDGE
BARLEY and OAT CAKES
BEEF (OCCASIONALLY) — SALTED FOR WINTER USE
WHISKY, ALE (CHIEFS DRANK WINE)

The chiefs sat in their castles, listening to their people's problems and sorting out their disputes. But everyone in the clan was equal and one Lowland visitor remarked . . .

In fact, just in case his kids got big ideas, it was common for a chief to foster out his children to ordinary clanspeople.

Not-so-important chiefs lived in turf houses like the tacksmen – those who leased land from the chief to farm. Then there were those who were a pain in the neck for everybody and owed allegiance to nobody – Cearnachs. They were bands of lawless men who were happy to do the odd shady deal.

Creachs, or cattle raids, were also a problem – but they were more of a sport than a crime as everybody got involved. One day you had cattle, the next day you hadn't, but you could always go and lift someone else's. Young men looked forward to the day when they could prove their manhood by going reiving.

A COUPLE OF HANDY HINTS TO EASE THE GRIEF OF CATTLE RAIDS:

SAVE YOUR SKINS (THE ONES ON THE HOOF) – PAY BLACK MAIL (A BRIBE) TO REIVERS AND THEY'LL LEAVE YOUR CATTLE ALONE (MAYBE).

MAKE A LITTLE FOR YOURSELF – DEMAND COLLOP MONEY FROM REIVERS IF THEY DRIVE STOLEN CATTLE ACROSS YOUR LANDS.

Cattle-reiving was nothing compared to the mayhem between the clans – feuds, duels, battles, burnings and all kinds of nastiness. Now that the Lords of the Isles had gone there was no one to keep the lid on things. Two new super-chiefs had appeared – the Earl of Argyll (chief of the Campbells) and the Earl of Huntly (head of the Gordons), but they were quite happy to secretly sponsor a few dastardly deeds if it was to their advantage.

MEANWHILE...
in the other part of Scotland...

KING JAMES V...

MARY QUEEN OF SCOTS...

AND JAMES VI...

WERE ALL CHILDREN WHEN THEY INHERITED THE KINGDOM. NO FIRM MANAGEMENT AT THE TOP MEANT A LOT OF UNRULY BEHAVIOUR FROM POWERFUL NOBLES. NOT MUCH DIFFERENT FROM THE HIGHLANDS, IN FACT.

By now, the Lowlanders saw the Highlanders as foreigners because:

Ⓐ THEY WORE STRANGE CLOTHES.
Ⓑ THEY SPOKE A STRANGE LANGUAGE. (GAELIC, ONCE SPOKEN THROUGHOUT MOST OF SCOTLAND, HAD BEEN REPLACED BY ENGLISH EVERYWHERE EXCEPT THE HIGHLANDS).

Scottish kings were getting fed up with the way the Highlands didn't play by the royal rules. James V sent an invitation to the chiefs:

To ALL HIGHLAND CHIEFS

Royal Cruise. My ship will pick you up at a port of your choice, for a mystery cruise through the Western Isles. Refusal is not an option.
yours James V (King)

65

The king took them up the Clyde to Dumbarton and thence to Edinburgh where they were interrogated. Some were let go after they made a promise of good behaviour. More awkward customers were imprisoned (and some were still there when the king died). James VI, on the other hand, wanted to . . .

...Plant a little civility in the Highlands.

The Highlands weren't uncivilised, they just did things differently. King James came up with some plans. Firstly, he demanded . . .

All chiefs must produce charters which prove they own their lands.

Now, many chiefs never had charters (official documents). It was also difficult to keep a charter if your home was often burnt down or your possessions kept getting stolen. A chief without a charter lost his land to the king.

I'm sure I had a bit of paper with something on it!

The plan didn't work very well, so James moved on.

> A CUNNING PLAN
> (A) – LOWLANDERS VERY CIVILISED.
> (B) – HIGHLANDERS VERY UNCIVILISED.
> THEREFORE...
> MOVE SOME OF (A) TO WHERE (B) LIVE AND...

> They will be given powers to root out the barbarous inhabitants.

How they did this was up to them. So a party of Lowlanders (known as the Fife Adventurers) set up farms on the island of Lewis. If this was successful, then similar schemes would be tried in other parts of the Highlands and – hey presto! – the Highlands would be a haven of peace. It was a disaster. the indignant locals soon had the Lowlanders running for their boats.

Then James drew up some rules . . .

RULES for CHIEFS

1. LESS WINE AND WHISKY TO BE CONSUMED.
2. CHIEFS TO CUT BACK ON THE LENGTH OF THEIR *TAIL* (i.e. LESS HANGERS-ON).
3. LIMIT QUANTITY OF ARMS CARRIED BY CLANSMEN.
4. SONS OF CHIEFS TO BE SENT TO LOWLANDS FOR GOOD EDUCATION (AND LEARN ENGLISH).
5. BARDS TO BE MADE REDUNDANT (THEY INFLAME HEROIC PASSION TOO MUCH).

Please sign here and return to me ....

James VI (King)

Then James had another idea or two . . .

ANOTHER CUNNING PLAN

1. CHIEFS TO PAY ME LOTS OF MONEY AS A GUARANTEE OF PEACEFUL BEHAVIOUR OF CLAN.
2. CHIEFS TO APPEAR BEFORE THE PRIVY COUNCIL IN EDINBURGH ONCE A YEAR TO GIVE US A RUN-DOWN ON WHAT'S HAPPENING.

James VI (King).

When the chiefs got to Ediburgh they were sometimes kept waiting for months. While they waited they began to enjoy the city life. The chiefs were going soft.

By now there were two religions in Scotland – the old Catholic one and the 'reformed church'. This new Protestant religion was for people who liked things simple – no bishops, no frills. However, King Charles I liked his religion with frills and expected his subjects to agree. Many Scots didn't want to be told how to worship. In protest, they signed a petition called the Covenant and they became known as Covenanters.

These were tricky times. You had to be very careful whose side you were on.

We're for the KING... or... er... maybe not.

Now the Highlands were feeling the effects of powerful men and their plans. Many of them didn't know which side they were on.

MONTROSE AND HIS FEW HUNDRED IRISHMEN WERE
DEFEATED BY AN ARMY OF COVENANTERS
AT THE BATTLE OF PHILIPHAUGH.
MONTROSE WAS EVENTUALLY EXECUTED
IN EDINBURGH AND HIS HEAD WAS
DISPLAYED ON A SPIKE OUTSIDE
THE TOLBOOTH.

GENERAL MONK

CHARLES I LOST THE CIVIL WAR AND HIS HEAD. OLIVER
CROMWELL RULED. HE SENT GENERAL MONK TO SCOTLAND
TO TIDY THINGS UP. TO KEEP THE PEACE, MONK BUILT
FIVE INTIMIDATING FORTRESSES.
TWO WERE IN THE HIGHLANDS-
ONE AT EACH END OF THE
GREAT GLEN.
MONK KNEW WHICH SIDE TO BE
ON. HE STARTED OFF AS A ROYALIST,
CHANGED OVER TO CROMWELL'S
SIDE THEN BACK AGAIN WHEN
CROMWELL DIED AND CHARLES
II WAS PROCLAIMED KING. THE
KING MADE HIM A DUKE.

FORT AT INVERNESS

GREAT GLEN

FORT AT INVERLOCHY
(IN GAELIC,
AN GEARASDAIN –
THE GARRISON)

THE 8TH EARL of ARGYLL

ARCHIBALD CAMPBELL* CHANGED
SIDES, TOO — BUT HE DIDN'T GET
IT QUITE RIGHT. HE STARTED OFF
AS A COVENANTER THEN
CHANGED HIS MIND.

Covenant?
King?
Covenant?
King?

* THE SAME EARL OF ARGYLL WHOSE
DINNER WAS INTERRUPTED BY MONTROSE.

NOW, THE SCOTS WERE IN A HUFF ABOUT CHARLES I's EXECUTION SO THEY INVITED HIS SON (WHO HAD BEEN LIVING ABROAD) TO BE THEIR KING. THE EARL OF ARGYLL PLACED THE CROWN ON KING CHARLES II's HEAD. CROMWELL WAS FURIOUS. CHARLES FLED ABROAD AGAIN. CROMWELL MADE ARGYLL SIGN AN OATH.

Suit you, Sire.

I promise to be good and I think O. Cromwell is a really good guy.

BUT THE KING WASN'T HAVING ANY OF THAT. AS FAR AS HE WAS CONCERNED, ARGYLL HAD BEEN CO-OPERATING WITH THE ENEMY. OFF TO THE TOWER OF LONDON WENT ARGYLL. CALL THE EXECUTIONER! ARGYLL'S HEAD WAS DISPLAYED OUTSIDE THE TOLBOOTH IN EDINBURGH.

WHEN CHARLES II RETURNED TO BE THE RIGHTFUL KING AFTER CROMWELL'S DEATH, ARGYLL RUSHED TO GREET HIM.

How nice to see you again, Sire!

Get rid of Montrose, John – we've got a nice fresh one here!

72

MEANWHILE ELSEWHERE...

KING CHARLES II DIED CHILDLESS SO HIS BROTHER BECAME KING AS JAMES II. (OR JAMES VII OF SCOTS.)

THIS GOT PEOPLE IN A FLAP BECAUSE JAMES WAS A CATHOLIC AND BRITAIN WAS OFFICIALLY A PROTESTANT COUNTRY. THEN, EVEN WORSE, JAMES' WIFE PRODUCED A SON AND HEIR—

JAMES FRANCIS EDWARD.

REMEMBER THIS BABY!

9TH EARL of ARGYLL

HE WAS A STAUNCH ROYALIST BUT ON THE OTHER HAND, HE REFUSED TO PUT HIS SIGNATURE TO A GOVERNMENT ACT WHICH OUTLAWED COVENANTERS. AN UNLIMITED STAY BEHIND BARS IN EDINBURGH WAS ARRANGED FOR HIS LACK OF CO-OPERATION. HE ESCAPED (DRESSED AS A MAID) AND FLED ABROAD WHERE HE CONSPIRED WITH THE DUKE OF MONMOUTH...

Look, Monmouth, we'll invade and I'll get my lands back!

PLOT, PLOT! SCHEME, SCHEME!

And I'll become King! A good Protestant one.

MONMOUTH LANDED IN ENGLAND WHILE THE EARL INVADED HIS HOME TERRITORY OF ARGYLL. HE CAPTURED A FEW CASTLES IN WHAT WAS KNOWN AS 'ARGYLL'S RISING'. THE RISING SOON SUNK. GOVERMENT SHIPS WERE SENT TO BLOW UP SOME OF ARGYLL'S CASTLES. THE EARL WAS CAUGHT AND SOON HIS HEAD REPLACED HIS DAD'S OUTSIDE THE TOLBOOTH.

Don't have much luck, these Argylls!

MEANWHILE... ELSEWHERE...

KING JAMES II (OR VII) BECAME VERY UNPOPULAR. HE MADE A QUICK EXIT...

... AND KING WILLIAM AND QUEEN MARY MADE A SWIFT ENTRANCE...

MARY WAS JAMES' DAUGHTER BY HIS FIRST MARRIAGE. SHE AND WILLIAM WERE INVITED BY PARLIAMENT TO BECOME KING AND QUEEN BECAUSE THEY WERE PROTESTANTS AND THEREFORE MUCH MORE TO THE COUNTRY'S LIKING.

VISCOUNT DUNDEE

JOHN GRAHAM OF CLAVERHOUSE WAS A HANDSOME AND DASHING SOLDIER.

HE WAS GIVEN TWO NICKNAMES - 'BONNIE DUNDEE' (BECAUSE OF HIS LOOKS) AND 'BLOODY CLAVERS' (BECAUSE OF BLOODTHIRSTY HABITS AS A SOLDIER).

ALTHOUGH HE HAD ONCE FOUGHT FOR WILLIAM (IN HOLLAND, BEFORE HE BECAME KING), DUNDEE NOW DECIDED TO STRIKE A BLOW FOR THE DEPARTED KING JAMES. HE GATHERED AN ARMY OF HIGHLANDERS BUT HE WAS MET BY GOVERNMENT FORCES LED BY GENERAL McKAY AT THE PASS OF KILLIECRANKIE.

THE HIGHLANDERS CHARGED AND McKAY'S TROOPS WERE ROUTED. POOR DUNDEE NEVER SAW THE VICTORY. HE WAS KILLED BY A MUSKET SHOT AT THE START OF THE BATTLE. THE HIGHLANDERS LOOTED THE ENEMY BODIES AND CAMP THEN WENT HOME.

SCOTLAND HAD NOW DIVIDED ITSELF INTO WILLIAMITES (THOSE WHO SUPPORTED KING WILLIAM) AND JACOBITES (THOSE WHO SUPPORTED EX-KING JAMES). SOMETIMES, LOYALTIES

> You're making a mistake, son!

CUT ACROSS FAMILIES. THE CHIEF OF THE CAMERONS WAS ON DUNDEE'S SIDE AT KILLIECRANKIE BUT HIS SON WAS A CAPTAIN IN McKAY'S ARMY. ALSO, THIS WAS A BATTLE

> So are you, Dad.

BETWEEN A HIGHLAND ARMY LED BY A LOWLANDER AND A LOWLAND ARMY LED BY A HIGHLANDER.

THE GOVERMENT WAS NOW A BIT JITTERY OVER THIS UNREST. GENERAL McKAY WAS ORDERED TO IMPROVE CROMWELL'S FORT AT INVERLOCHY. SOLDIERS COULD THEN BE GARRISONED THERE TO KEEP AN EYE ON THE HIGHLANDS. THE NEW FORTIFICATIONS WERE NAMED 'FORT WILLIAM' IN HONOUR OF THE KING. BUT AN EXTRA MEASURE WAS NEEDED TO KEEP THE HIGHLANDS UNDER CONTROL...

> I will take 7,000 Troops through the Highlands to the fort as a show of strength.

PLAN: FORT WILLIAM

JOHN CAMPBELL, EARL of BREADALBANE and JOHN DALRYMPLE, EARL of STAIR

BREADALBANE WAS DESCRIBED AS BEING AS CUNNING AS A FOX, WISE AS A SERPENT AND SLIPPERY AS AN EEL. STAIR WAS CRAFTY AND UNSCRUPULOUS.

THEY WERE BOTH SUSPECTED OF JACOBITE TENDENCIES BUT THEY EAGERLY SERVED KING WILLIAM. BREADALBANE WAS GIVEN THE TASK OF DISTRIBUTING MONEY TO THE HIGHLAND CHIEFS IN RETURN FOR LOYALTY. PERHAPS THE BRIBES NEVER REACHED THE CHIEFS...

How was the money distributed, Breadalbane?

The Highlands are quiet, the money has been spent and that is the only way of accounting between friends.

BUT THE HIGHLANDS WERE NOT QUIET SO THE GOVERNMENT ISSUED A PROCLAMATION:

To All Highland Chiefs

You must all swear allegiance to King William III by 1st of January 1692 or face the consequences.

ALL CHIEFS SIGNED ON TIME EXCEPT MACDO[...]
GLENCOE. HE WAS JUST A LITTLE LATE IN GETTING [...]
SIGNING-PLACE. THE EARL OF STAIR, SECRETARY OF ST[...]
FOR SCOTLAND, DECIDED TO MAKE AN EXAMPLE OF
MACDONALD.

> The winter-time is the only
> season in which we are sure
> the Highlanders cannot
> escape. The long, dark nights
> is the time to maul them.

A REGIMENT OF CAMPBELL SOLDIERS ARRIVED AT THE
MACDONALD VILLAGE, CLAIMING UNABLE TO REACH FORT
WILLIAM IN THE BAD WEATHER. HIGHLAND HOSPITALITY
ENSURED THEY WERE WELCOMED INTO MACDONALD HOMES.

> At the signal, put all to the
> sword under 70. Make special
> care the chief and his sons
> do not escape.

THE CAMPBELLS STRUCK. THE MACDONALD WAS
MURDERED IN HIS BED. HIS WIFE'S RINGS WERE GNAWED
FROM HER FINGERS BY A SOLDIER. 38 MACDONALDS
WERE KILLED, THEIR HOUSES TORCHED. MANY ESCAPED
INTO THE ICY DARKNESS OF SNOW-COVERED MOUNTAINS.

THE CENTURY ENDED
IN THE HIGHLANDS
WITH A MASSACRE
THAT SHOOK THE
WHOLE
NATION.

...e MacDonalds by Campbells in ...adlines, but it wasn't the first (or the worst) bloodshed between the two clans. They had been at each other's throats for centuries. The first victim of this long feud was probably Colin Campbell (a.k.a. Big Colin or Chailean Mor) who was murdered by a MacDougall (distant cousins of the MacDonalds) in 1296.

Now the MacDonalds looked on Argyll as their own patch so when Campbells began to muscle in and build a castle (Inchconnel) on a island on Loch Awe, they were not too pleased.

The MacDonalds kept a grip on their territory with good old-fashioned bully-boy tactics – raids, burnings, nifty sword-play etc. The Campbells were much more subtle. They always sucked up to whichever king was around and it usually paid off with rewards of titles, lands and castles. Campbell lands began to spread while MacDonald lands shrunk. The MacDonalds fought back but without much success as the Campbells became Earls, then Marquises, and finally Dukes of Argyll.

In the next chapter, Highlanders battle against boots and buttons, a sad Stuart pretends he's prepared, prepared prince realises his rebellion is rotten.

The Time of Rebellion

FROM ABOUT 1700

The new century began but the Highlanders couldn't put away their weapons just yet. There were still problems to sort out.

LOCHABER AXE

TARGE MADE OF LAYERS OF WOOD WITH LEATHER COVERING

CLAIDHEAMH DA LAIMH (TWO-HANDED SWORD)

CLAIDHEAMH MOR (CLAYMORE)

GUN POWDER HORN

DIRK

PISTOL

One problem was the increasing discipline of the enemy.

Oliver Cromwell had realised that if you wanted a proper army, you wouldn't get it by asking the farmer or the baker to down tools and pick up a sword (old style). You needed professional, well-drilled soldiers who got paid for the job they did (new style). So this was what the Highlanders had to face now and most of them still fought with bows and arrows and axes, and they were barefoot, too. However, the traditional down-hill, whooping, charge of the Highlanders still struck terror into professional soldiers.

MEANWHILE...
ELSEWHERE...

KING WILLIAM & QUEEN MARY DIED. MARY'S SISTER, ANNE, BECAME QUEEN.

THE SCOTTISH PARLIAMENT WAS CLOSED DOWN. FROM NOW ON, DECISIONS WERE MADE IN LONDON. SCOTS WERE NOT PLEASED.

Bought and sold for English gold!

ANNE DIED. NO KIDS. A DISTANT RELATIVE WAS CHOSEN AS NEXT KING — GEORGE OF HANOVER.

The Jacobites decided that this was not on. The Stewart dynasty had more claim to the throne than a gent from Germany who couldn't even speak English. The Jacobites met in France and plotted.

Now that ex-king James VII was dead, they felt that James Francis Edward Stuart (yes, it's that baby, now aged 19) was the rightful king of Great Britain, so . . .

PLAN No. 1 ~ 1708

King Louis XIV of France was not on speaking terms with his English neighbours so, just to irritate them, he agreed to support the Jacobites.

Ships were supplied to take James to Scotland. Supporters were waiting there, ready to gather an army.

English ships stopped the French ships getting anywhere near the Scottish coast. James was not a good sailor and was just recovering from the measles.

The incident gave the government in London the jitters. They thought they saw Jacobites everywhere.

PLAN No. 2 ~ 1715

The Earl of Mar had been a government official in London until he was given the sack. He returned home to Scotland to huff and to plot. He organised a hunt in Braemar. When the nobles gathered on the hillside, it wasn't deer they had come to stalk. They had come to hear Mar's plot.

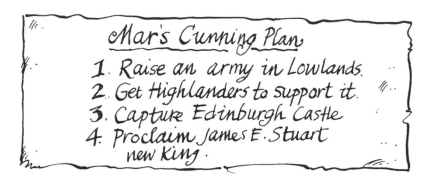

Mar's Cunning Plan

1. Raise an army in Lowlands.
2. Get Highlanders to support it.
3. Capture Edinburgh Castle.
4. Proclaim James E. Stuart new King.

James's ships made preparations to sail to Scotland again. Mar gathered an army and managed to capture Perth, Aberdeen and Inverness. However, he failed to get Edinburgh in his shopping basket. 12,000 clansmen joined him and he met the government army at Sheriffmuir.

FAILURE No 2.

James had arrived at Peterhead. He hung around in the bleak winter weather for a few weeks then went back to France.

The Battle of Sheriffmuir was a draw but because Mar led his team off the pitch first, he was regarded as the loser. In the local taverns, the punters had a new song to sing about the battle.

The government in London got more jittery than ever. Regiments of soldiers set up camp on the outskirts of the city, just in case. The government dished out punishments.

MEMO ~   Things to do with Jacobites

1   If they're rich enough to have estates, confiscate them.
2.   If they're poor, pack 'em off to America as slaves... er... for a long stay.
3.   Execute a few, just to show we mean business.

But the Jacobites didn't give up.

PLAN No.3 ~ 1719

Spanish help. A Spanish fleet had recently been attacked by English ships. The Spanish were looking for revenge. The agreed to send a fleet with 5,000 troops to invade England. At the same time the Jacobites were to organise a rebellion in Scotland. James went to Spain to be picked up by the Spanish and brought to Britain.

I'm ready.

FAILURE No. 3

A storm scattered the
Spanish fleet and they
returned to port. James
decided to give up trying
to be king.

At the Scottish end of the operation, things didn't go any
better. The two commanders, the Earl Marischal and
the Earl of Tullibardine, arrived by ship at Eilean Donan
Castle near the island of Skye.

Two commanders – two different plans – no agreements –
one big disaster. Few Highlanders came to join the jaunt,
which was finished when English ships arrived . . .

The government in London had yet another attack of the jitters.

Something had to be done about this bad habit the Highlanders had of supporting the Jacobite upstart. Step forward, General George Wade.

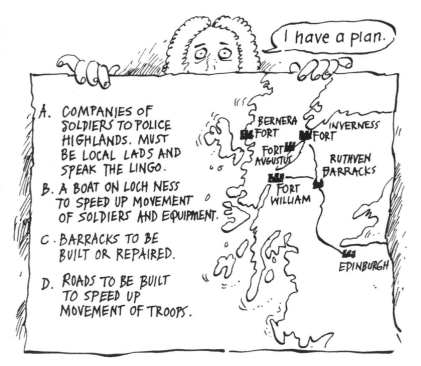

First you see them, then you don't. The Highlanders were experts at just disappearing into the mountains they knew so well. They didn't need roads but government troops did. Roads were going to change the look of the Highlands forever. Wade had 400km of roads and around 40 bridges built. Fort George (named in honour of the King) was built at Inverness.

The Design for a FORT at INVERNESS to be built on the site of an ancient castle.

He named Fort Augustus after one of the King's sons. (We'll meet Augustus again.)

The design for a FORT at KILCHUMEN to be renamed FORT AUGUSTUS.

RULES for RUTHVEN BARRACKS
1. ONLY TEN MEN PER ROOM.
2. TWO MEN PER BED.
3. MEN MUST COOK THEIR OWN FOOD, DO THEIR OWN LAUNDRY AND CLEANING.
4. CANDLES AND COAL WILL BE PROVIDED FOR EACH MAN.

PLAN No.4 ~ 1745

James Stuart had gone off to put his feet up in Italy
and had lost interest in being a king. His son decided
it was worth another try. He was twenty-five, athletic,
energetic and liked to party. He was Charles Edward
Louis John Casimir Silvester Severino Mario Stuart –
better known as Bonnie Prince Charlie.

He pawned the family jewels and borrowed some money
from a Scottish banker in Paris.

Charles set sail from France and headed for the west
of Scotland.

My Cunning Plan

1. Land on West Coast of Scotland.
2. Highland clans will flock to join my army.
3. French will invade England from south.
4. English Jacobites will come to join us.
5. Proclaim Dad king James VIII

Things went wrong right away. One of the ships was lost (the one with most of the arms and the soldiers, of course). The Prince landed on the island of Eriskay in the Outer Hebrides and met problem number two – many of the chiefs were lukewarm about joining in the fun. Charles said to one of them . . .

I am determined to display my standard and take to the field with whoever may join me. You may stay at home and learn your Prince's fate from the newspapers.

Prince Charles Edward Stuart raises standard at Glenfinnan

The Prince, who claims the British throne for his father, said the clans were rushing to support his cause.

In fact, only some of the clans joined Charles. Many weren't too keen on losing their lands, their fortunes and maybe their heads, if things went wrong. Some of them hedged their bets.

Wade's Forts and Roads no Hindrance to Charlie!

The forts that General Wade built to control the Highlands are so poorly garrisoned that they have been unable to stop the Prince's march east. The roads have helped the Highland army speed on its way!

Prince Pushes On! Cope Confused!

Citizens of Edinburgh found themselves in Jacobite hands this morning after the Prince and his supporters gained entry into the city when the gates were opened after dark to admit a wagon. General Cope, commanding government troops, ended up in Inverness after taking a wrong turning. He is quickly returning south by sea with the intention of retaking Edinburgh.

General Cope arrived at Dunbar and the Prince took his army out to meet them.

The Daily Gossip   *September 1745*

Prince Pans Raw Recruits at Prestonpans!

These Highlanders scare the pants off me!

Cope's young, untrained conscripts were terrified and trounced by the Highland army at the battle yesterday.

Now the Prince had won Scotland but his eyes were set on bigger prey – why not England, too? He decided to wait a while in the hope that more clansmen might join him. Young ladies from Edinburgh were taking carriages out to the army camp in the hope of catching a glimpse of the dashing prince.

The Daily Gossip   *October 1745*

Palace Parties For Prince!

The dust-covers have been thrown off the furniture in Holyrood Palace, Edinburgh, as Prince Charles dances the night away. Every lady there received a commemorative fan.

THE PRINCE'S PROGRESS

ERISKAY
SKYE
CULLODEN
INVERNESS
GLEN FINNAN
PERTH
PRESTONPANS
GLASGOW
EDINBURGH
CARLISLE
MANCHESTER
DERBY
LONDON

THE DAILY GOSSIP
THE PRINCE'S
PROGRESS
FULL ANALYSIS
INSIDE

Charles decided to march into England though his army commanders weren't too keen. Some of the Highlanders were even less keen on crossing the border and drifted off home. It spite of this, the march was easy.

The Daily Gossip   *December 1745*

Prince's Army at Derby!!

The Jacobite army has reached Derby and be in London in two days. The city is in panic. The king's yacht lies in the Thames ready to evacuate King George if necessary. Many citizens are selling up and moving out!

Derby resident bitter about billeting.

I've had to take in 14 of those Highland louts. They sleep on hay in front of the fire. They smell. They will infest the house with fleas!

But at Derby there was a hiccup in the Prince's smooth progress. Where was the French invasion fleet? Nowhere. Where were the English Jacobites who were going to swell the numbers of the Prince's army? Nowhere. Nevertheless, the Prince wanted to press on towards London. His commanders disagreed. Who knows what lay before them? Step forward one Dudley Bradstreet!

This helpful chappie had information . . .

There is a government army of 9,000 men blocking the route to London!

That was all Charles's commanders wanted to hear. The army was ordered to turn round and head back north. Mr Bradstreet was, in fact, a government spy. He had lied. The government troops were at that moment marching into Scotland.

The Daily Gossip   *February 1746*

Prince Pushes Off Home.

THE EMERGENCY IS OVER!
Londoners can sleep safely in their beds once more. The Jacobite army has returned to Scotland. Having been given the cold shoulder by Glasgow, the Prince has continued to Inverness.

Would you believe it? He's asked Glasgow to provide clothes for his entire army!!

Charles couldn't rest at Inverness. A government army was fast approaching led by Augustus (yes, *that* Augustus), Duke of Cumberland, soon to be known as 'Butcher Cumberland' (we'll soon find out why). He was the same age as Charles but a good deal fatter.

The last battle ever to be fought on British soil was about to take place.

On one side, the Highland army, exhausted, starved, diseased and out-numbered 2 to 1. On the other side, the government troops (plus clans, too) – well trained and well equipped.

The Daily Gossip   *April 1746*

CARNAGE AT CULLODEN!

Today, the rebel Jacobite army faced the forces of the Duke of Cumberland (and sleet-laden north-east wind) on the moor at Culloden. The ground

between the two armies was rough and boggy and not what one of the rebel commanders, Lord Murray, would have liked. It is said that many of the Highlanders were away foraging for food

when the order for the charge was given. The battle was all over within half an hour and the Highland army was decimated. When the

defeat became obvious, Prince Charles urged his men to retreat. No one now knows where the Prince has gone.

Posters went up around the country.

The Duke of Cumberland now gained his nickname of 'The Butcher'.

Anyone found alive on the battlefield was slaughtered (including some schoolboys who had come out from Inverness to watch the battle). The Duke and his men rampaged through the glens, destroying everything in their path.

Houses were burnt (preferably with the owners inside), livestock driven off, boats smashed. Jacobite chiefs lost their lands and their heads. Hundreds of clansfolk were transported to America as slaves.

Even more roads appeared in the Highlands. A huge, new Fort George was built at Inverness. Thousands of men with spades and buckets worked to build the mighty ramparts. It was hi-tech and designed to terrify.

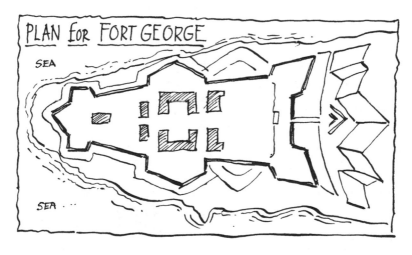

Someone in the government even suggested that the Highlands ought to be completely cleared of inhabitants. They could all be packed off to America and replaced with nicer people! In fact, the government couldn't quite get rid of the Highlanders, but it could try and make them invisible . . .

IMPORTANT NOTICE
TO ALL HIGHLAND PERSONS

FROM NOW ON THE FOLLOWING ITEMS ARE BANNED:

1) HIGHLAND CLOTHES, PLAID, TREWS OR ANY TARTAN OR CHECKED CLOTH.
2) GUNS, SWORDS, DIRKS, PISTOLS OR ANY OTHER WEAPON.
3) THE PLAYING OF BAGPIPES.

1ST. OFFENCE : SIX MONTHS IN PRISON.
2ND. OFFENCE : SEVEN YEARS TRANSPORTATION.

Castles throughout the Highlands were turned into army barracks so that government soldiers (called Redcoats, because of their scarlet uniforms) could patrol the glens and make sure the Highlanders were behaving. No doubt some Highlanders gave the soldiers a hard time.

Hey! Come and get me!

Prince Charles was also being a bit of a tease. He was desperately waiting for a French ship to take him to safety. For five months he was on the run. Round and round the Highlands and islands he went, trying to keep out of the clutches of the soldiers who were stalking him. It was a time of rough living and narrow escapes.

18TH CENTURY JOKE — CHARLES AS FLORA MACDONALD'S MAID 'BETTY BURKE'!

CHARLES WAS KNOWN TO HIS ENEMIES AS THE 'YOUNG PRETENDER' AND HIS FATHER WAS KNOWN AS THE 'OLD PRETENDER' – A PRETENDER WAS SOMEONE WHO CLAIMED SOMETHING (IN THIS CASE, A CROWN). SO, AT ONE POINT IN HIS ADVENTURES – WHEN CHARLES HAD TO DISGUISE HIMSELF AS A LADY'S MAID – ONE OF HIS COMPANIONS JOKED "THAT'S THE WORST PRETENDER I'VE EVER SEEN!" (HO-HO-HO!)

Many in the Highlands could have shopped Charles and claimed the reward, but none did. Charles eventually got his ship. He retired to Italy, took to drink and became flabby and bored. The Jacobite adventure died with him.

**MEANWHILE...
ELSEWHERE...**

A GREAT CHANGE WAS TAKING OVER THE COUNTRY. IT WAS CALLED THE INDUSTRIAL REVOLUTION. STEAMPOWER HAD BEEN INVENTED AND THIS COULD DRIVE ALL SORTS OF MACHINERY.

THE FIRST FACTORIES WERE BEING BUILT. A CANAL WAS BEING CONSTRUCTED THAT WOULD CARRY SHIPS ACROSS THE MIDDLE OF SCOTLAND. THE HIGHLANDS WOULD SOON FEEL THE EFFECTS OF ALL THIS.

A great change had also taken over the chiefs. Once upon a time they were the fathers of the clan. They were leaders and equals.

Now they were landowners and clanspeople couldn't expect something for nothing.

A lot of chiefs no longer lived on their Highland estates. They employed someone else – the Factor – to do the dirty work.

Another strange change was taking place. Suddenly, people elsewhere were taking an interest in the Highlands. This usually meant they wanted something. People elsewhere wanted more and more of the Highlanders' cattle. They wanted timber and fish and stone. Slate and granite quarries appeared on the islands, providing materials for distant, growing cities.

NOT LONG AFTER THE LAST JACOBITE REBELLION, AN IRON FURNACE WAS BUILT AT BONAWE IN ARGYLL. THERE HAD BEEN FURNACES IN THE HIGHLANDS BEFORE BUT THIS ONE WAS ON A GRANDER SCALE. IRON WORKS NEEDED WOOD (FUEL), WATER (POWER) AND WATER (TRANSPORT). THE HIGHLANDS HAD PLENTY OF THOSE. THE IRON ORE WAS BROUGHT FROM CENTRAL SCOTLAND FOR PROCESSING AT BONAWE.

The air on the islands smelled of burnt seaweed (called kelp). Seaweed ash was needed in the manufacture of glass and soap and for bleaching linen. Well, the islands had tons of the stuff. It was cut at low tide, piled in pits on the beach and burnt with peat.

MOST HIGHLANDERS WERE FARMERS. THEY GREW THEIR OWN FOOD, TENDED THEIR ANIMALS, WOVE CLOTH TO MAKE THEIR CLOTHES. THEIR HOUSES SAT IN SMALL CLUSTERS. THERE WERE FEW VILLAGES AND TOWNS LIKE THOSE IN THE LOWLANDS.

NOW, THE 3RD DUKE OF ARGYLL WANTED TO BUILD HIMSELF A SMART NEW CASTLE IN THE LATEST STYLE. THIS GAVE HIM A GOOD EXCUSE TO GET RID OF ALL THE HOUSES OF HIS TENANTS WHICH CROWDED ROUND HIS OLD CASTLE.

INVERARAY CASTLE BEGAN 1745 – TOOK 40 YEARS TO FINISH

HE BUILT NEW HOMES FOR HIS TENANTS, TOO – THE TOWN OF INVERARAY. IT IS KNOWN AS A 'PLANNED TOWN' BECAUSE IT WAS DESIGNED AND BUILT ALL IN ONE GO. OTHER SUCH TOWNS BEGAN TO APPEAR IN THE HIGHLANDS – SOME WERE BUILT FOR CERTAIN TRADESPEOPLE, LIKE FISHERMEN OR WEAVERS.

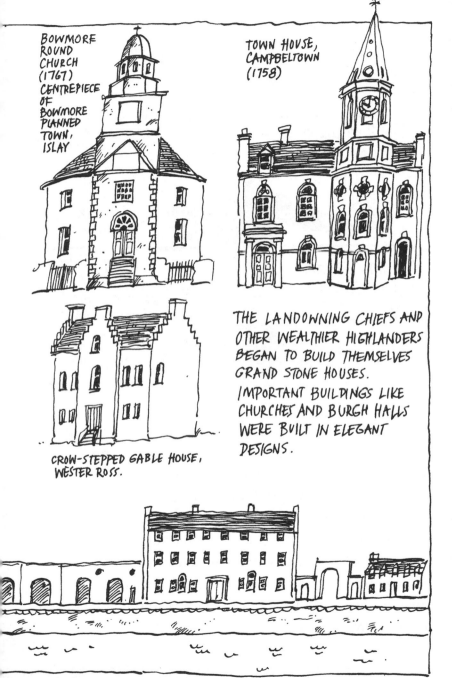

BOWMORE ROUND CHURCH (1767) CENTREPIECE OF BOWMORE PLANNED TOWN, ISLAY

TOWN HOUSE, CAMPBELTOWN (1758)

CROW-STEPPED GABLE HOUSE, WESTER ROSS.

THE LANDOWNING CHIEFS AND OTHER WEALTHIER HIGHLANDERS BEGAN TO BUILD THEMSELVES GRAND STONE HOUSES. IMPORTANT BUILDINGS LIKE CHURCHES AND BURGH HALLS WERE BUILT IN ELEGANT DESIGNS.

What the government wanted from the Highlands, above all, was men. They soon came up with a crafty new idea . . .

Army regiments of Highlanders now went off to scare the living daylights out of British enemies around the world. The Highland problem now was that there were just too many people, and not enough work to go round. Men and women began drifting away. They could go away for a season to help with the harvests in the lowlands. They could go away for longer, to work in the new textile factories in the cities. They could go away for ever, taking ship for America in the hope of a better life.

Yet another strange change had taken place. For centuries, Lowlanders had seen the Highlands as an ugly, wild place. Now, it was a place of romantic beauty in their eyes. Poets and artists packed their notepads and paints and came to faint with delight at the views. The first tourists had arrived. This didn't do much for the locals. No more seaweed ash was needed, as a cheaper product could be brought from abroad. Highlanders who earned a living from kelp-burning were at a loss. Now something even more deadly than Redcoats was about to appear in the glens and make the Highlanders' lives a misery. It was called the SHEEP.

In the next chapter: cows can't compete with walking wool, Highlanders herded onto soggy ships, awkward activists make the Sheriff scream.

The Time of Clearance

FROM ABOUT 1800

The Highlanders' cattle were their most valuable possessions.

GOOD THINGS ABOUT THE COW

AT THIS END, EATS ALL SORTS OF GRASS

TRANSPORTS ITSELF TO MARKET

AT THIS END, PRODUCES MILK FOR BUTTER AND CHEESE

A THIS END, PRODUCES GOOD MUCK WHICH ENRICHES THE SOIL

Once a year, in early autumn, the Highlanders and their cattle went for a long walk. From all corners of the Highlands and Islands they came, along ancient routes known as drove roads. When they reached a narrow stretch of water the cattle had to swim. Islanders herded their beasts onto open boats to get across wider waters.

Hundreds of drovers and thousands of cattle arrived at the great Tryst (cattle market) at Falkirk. Here, deals would be done, gossip gathered, world events heard about and gifts bought.

The Highlanders had sheep, too, but they were delicate creatures that had to be given shelter at night. Now a new type of sheep had been brought to the Highlands. The landowners began to take a close interest. If there had been junk mail in those days, it might have looked like this . . .

DO YOU WANT TO INCREASE YOUR £££?

DO YOU SEEK IMPROVED PROFIT?

THEN READ THIS CAREFULLY!

OLD-STYLE HIGHLAND SHEEP — NEEDS CONSTANT LOOKING-AFTER. NEEDS TO BE PENNED AT NIGHT. DELICATE ANIMAL. FLEECE THIN.

NEW-STYLE. THE BLACKFACED AND CHEVIOT SHEEP WILL STAY ON HILLS ALL YEAR ROUND. TAKES EVERYTHING WEATHER CAN THROW AT IT. FLEECE THICK AND PLENTIFUL.

SEND AWAY FOR FREE TRIAL-PACK NOW!

But the new sheep had a downside, too . . .

And they needed large areas of land to live on . . .

The landowners were faced with a choice . . .

The landowners needed money to keep their estates ticking over, so they opted for sheep. A fat cow was a valuable cow. The Highlanders fattened their beasts on the lush grass of the hills during the summer before taking them to market. Now, the hills were out of bounds.

The Highlanders had lost their main source of earnings – and worse was to come.

The people were given a choice, but it wasn't much of a choice.

QUESTIONNAIRE for TENANTS

<u>TICK **ONE** BOX ONLY</u>
NOW THAT I AM TO BE REMOVED FROM MY FARM,
I WOULD LIKE:

[A] TO BE RESETTLED ON A WINDY, ROCKY, LITTLE
    BIT OF LAND BY THE SEA.
[B] TO BE SENT TO AMERICA/CANADA/AUSTRALIA.

Those who stayed were given meagre bits of land which became known as crofts. Woe betide any tenants who gathered bracken for thatch or let their horses graze on the landlord's ground! Those who chose to leave were herded onto rotten old ships (good ships were kept for important things, like tea, coffee or tobacco). Many ships full of people fell to bits in the middle of the Atlantic.

KING GEORGE IV PAID A VISIT TO EDINBURGH – THE FIRST MONARCH TO COME TO SCOTLAND IN 171 YEARS.

HE DRESSED FROM HEAD TO TOE IN TARTAN (PLUS PINK TIGHTS). THE LORD MAYOR OF LONDON CAME WITH HIM, DRESSED LIKEWISE. TARTAN, KILTS AND SPORRANS WERE SUDDENLY ALL THE RAGE...

Queen Victoria and her husband Albert arrived. They bought a little property near Braemar for holidays. The countryside reminded Albert of his home in Germany.

Victoria put up tartan curtains in her holiday home at Balmoral Castle. She set a trend. Everything Highland became fashionable, and landowners were soon building themselves fairy-tale castles in the glens.

THE HIGHLANDS - A ROMANTIC HIT!

A SCHOOLMASTER CALLED JAMES MACPHERSON PUBLISHED A BOOK OF POEMS WHICH HE CLAIMED WERE WRITTEN BY THE CELTIC BARD, OSSIAN (WHO PERHAPS LIVED AROUND 200AD).

THE BOOK WAS A BEST-SELLER THROUGHOUT EUROPE AND AMERICA. THE POEMS TURNED OUT TO BE FAKES — BUT READERS WERE HOOKED BY THE ROMANTIC HIGHLANDS THEY HAD READ ABOUT IN THE BOOK.

MANY OF THE NOVELS BY SIR WALTER SCOTT WERE SET IN SCOTLAND.

HIS BOOKS WERE ALSO KEENLY READ THROUGHOUT EUROPE. PEOPLE LIKED THE BEAUTIFUL, WILD AND DRAMATIC IMAGE OF SCOTLAND HE PORTRAYED IN HIS BOOKS.

PAINTERS WERE GETTING IN ON THE ACT, TOO.

E. LANDSEER - THE STAG AT BAY

Meanwhile, life carried on for the Highlanders . . .

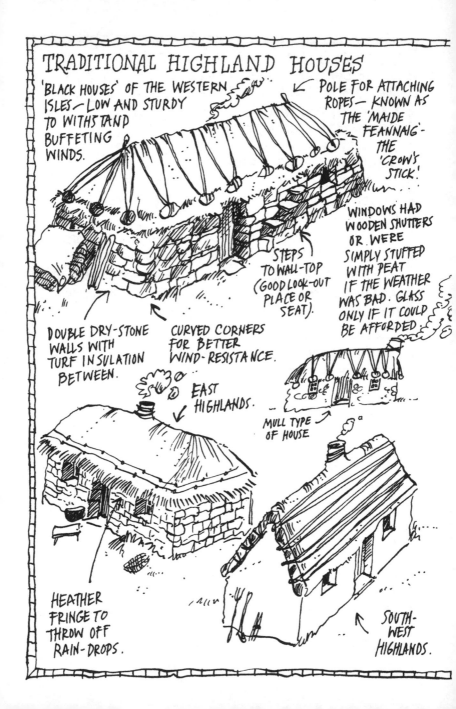

TRADITIONAL HIGHLAND HOUSES

'BLACK HOUSES' OF THE WESTERN ISLES — LOW AND STURDY TO WITHSTAND BUFFETING WINDS.

POLE FOR ATTACHING ROPES — KNOWN AS THE 'MAIDE FEANNAIG' — THE 'CROW'S STICK'!

WINDOWS HAD WOODEN SHUTTERS OR WERE SIMPLY STUFFED WITH PEAT IF THE WEATHER WAS BAD. GLASS ONLY IF IT COULD BE AFFORDED

STEPS TO WALL-TOP (GOOD LOOK-OUT PLACE OR SEAT).

DOUBLE DRY-STONE WALLS WITH TURF INSULATION BETWEEN.

CURVED CORNERS FOR BETTER WIND-RESISTANCE.

EAST HIGHLANDS.

MULL TYPE OF HOUSE

HEATHER FRINGE TO THROW OFF RAIN-DROPS.

SOUTH-WEST HIGHLANDS.

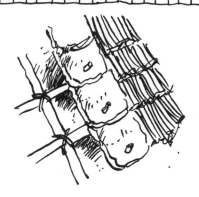

ROOF MADE OF A WOODEN
FRAMEWORK. TURF LAID
ON TOP THEN HELD IN PLACE
BY PEGS OF HEATHER TWIGS.
THATCH LAID ON TOP OF
THAT (BARLEY STRAW,
HEATHER, BRACKEN OR RUSHES)
HELD DOWN BY WEIGHTED
ROPES.

THATCH WAS REPLACED ONCE A YEAR. OLD THATCH WAS
USED ON FIELDS AS FERTILIZER.

STORE

BYRE

LIVING
AREA

HOUSES USUALLY HAD TWO
AREAS — ON FOR THE CATTLE,
ONE FOR HUMANS — DIVIDED
BY A PARTITION OF TURF OR
WOOD.
(IT HELPED TO HAVE THE HOUSE
SLOPING DOWN TOWARDS
THE BYRE!!)

EVERY SO OFTEN, THE BYRE'S
END WALL WAS KNOCKED
DOWN SO THAT THE COW-
MUCK COULD BE REMOVED.

THE FLOOR WAS OF COMPACTED
EARTH SOMETIMES COVERED
WITH MATS OR RUSHES.

OFTEN NO CHIMNEY — JUST A
HOLE IN ROOF — SO VERY
SMOKY INSIDE.

SNIGHE —
RAIN-DROPS
THAT FELL
FROM THE
THE
THATCH
INSIDE
WERE A
NUISANCE —

USUALLY
BLACK
BECAUSE
OF SOOT
ON
INSIDE
IF
ROOF.

What do you do with lots of ancient, squashed
dead plants? It's called peat and the Highlanders
used it for fuel. (Given a few extra million years
and a lot more squashing, it would have turned
into coal.) Cutting the peat began in April. It was
a job for the whole family and the neighbours,
and there was a holiday atmosphere at peat-
cutting time. A family had to cut enough peat to
last a year (as well as some for elderly relatives).

HOW TO CUT AND PREPARE PEAT

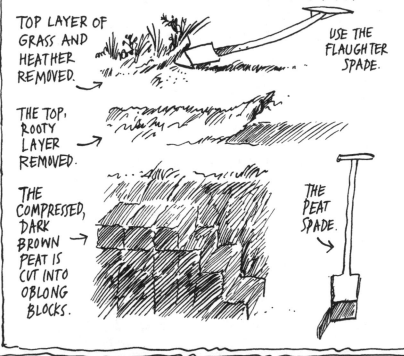

TOP LAYER OF
GRASS AND
HEATHER
REMOVED.

USE THE
FLAUGHTER
SPADE.

THE TOP,
ROOTY
LAYER
REMOVED.

THE
COMPRESSED,
DARK
BROWN
PEAT IS
CUT INTO
OBLONG
BLOCKS.

THE
PEAT
SPADE.

THE CUT PEATS WERE TOSSED ONTO THE HEATHER THEN STACKED TO DRY OUT.

AS THE PEAT BANKS WERE OFTEN IN THE MIDDLE OF NOWHERE, THE PEAT HAD TO BE CARRIED TO THE NEAREST TRACK THEN LOADED ONTO A HORSE-DRAWN CART.

PEAT BARROW

BACK HOME, THE PEAT WAS PILED INTO A HUGE HEAP (OFTEN AS BIG AS A HOUSE) VERY CAREFULLY SO THE RAIN WOULD RUN OFF AND THE PEATS WOULD REMAIN DRY.

What do you do if the ground on your croft is so rocky that there's hardly any soil to grow things in? You create Lazy Beds.

YOU USED A CAS CHROM (FOOT PLOUGH) TO TURN OVER THE THIN SOIL. THEN YOU BUILT A LOW WALL OF TURF AND FILLED INSIDE WITH SEAWEED.

THEN YOU PLANTED POTATOES IN THE BEDS.

HIGHLAND DIET
(IT HADN'T CHANGED MUCH FOR CENTURIES)
MILK – BUTTER – CHEESE.   POTATOES.
EGGS– EITHER FROM HENS OR SEABIRDS.
PORRIDGE OATS – EATEN FROM A WOODEN BOWL WITH A HORN SPOON.
BANNOCKS (FLAT CAKES) MADE FROM OAT- OR BARLEYMEAL
KALE (LEAFY VEGETABLE) OR WILD PLANTS– e.g. NETTLES (MADE INTO SOUP) – BERRIES.
SOMETIMES FISH OR MEAT (SOMETIMES POACHED FROM THE LANDLORD'S ESTATE).

Things couldn't get any worse for the Highlanders, could they? Oh yes they could! A disease called blight attacked their potatoes. The crofters watched their main food crop die. The stench of rotting spuds filled the air. Another wave of people packed their few belongings and boarded ships. Perhaps a life in Canada or Australia would be better than starvation.

A NEW TYPE OF LANDOWNER WAS ARRIVING IN THE HIGHLANDS.

BLAM!

THEY CAME FROM THE LOWLANDS AND ENGLAND. IF THEY DIDN'T FILL THEIR ESTATES WITH SHEEP, THEY TURNED THEM INTO DEER PARKS — MONEY COULD BE EARNED FROM OFFERING DEER-STALKING OR GROUSE-SHOOTING.

What else can you do to prevent your family starving to death? There were too many mouths to feed and the croft no longer supplied enough food to feed them. Crofters and their families had to find extra work.

FISHING

ALTHOUGH THE PEOPLE OF THE WEST OF SCOTLAND WERE SURROUNDED BY SEAS AND LOCHS, NOT MANY OF THEM WENT FISHING. THE SEAS WERE ROUGH AND THERE WEREN'T MANY HARBOURS, SO BOATS HAD TO BE PULLED UP ON THE BEACH. WOMEN SOMETIMES CARRIED THE MEN OUT TO THEIR BOATS ONCE THEY WERE LAUNCHED. THIS MEANT THAT THE FISHERMEN DIDN'T START A FISHING TRIP WITH WET CLOTHES.

BUT NOW FISHING BECAME VERY SUCCESSFUL IN SOME PARTS. AT CERTAIN TIMES, 500 OR 600 BOATS COULD BE SEEN ON LOCH FYNE FISHING FOR HERRING. 200 HORSES A DAY WERE NEEDED TO CARRY THE FISH AWAY.

LOCH FYNE FISHING-SKIFF—ALSO USED FOR RACING.

WEAVING

THE HIGHLAND PEOPLE HAD ALWAYS WOVEN CLOTH TO MAKE THEIR CLOTHES. NOW THEY BOUGHT THEIR CLOTHES BUT SPUN AND WOVE TO MAKE SOME EXTRA MONEY.

SPINNING WOOL INTO THREAD WITH A DISTAFF AND SPINDLE ← MEANT YOU COULD DO OTHER THINGS AT THE SAME TIME. THE SPINNING-WHEEL WAS QUICKER.

TWEED-MAKING WAS ENCOURAGED ON THE ISLAND OF HARRIS BY SOME LANDOWNERS' WIVES. TWEED BECAME A VERY FASHIONABLE CLOTH. THE NAME TWEED WAS PERHAPS TWILL OR TWEEL (A KIND OF WEAVING PATTERN) BUT SOMEONE ONCE WROTE THE WORD DOWN WRONGLY AND THE NAME STUCK.

WOOL WAS DYED IN THE OPEN AIR BY ← ADDING LEAVES, BARK, ROOTS OR FLOWERS TO THE BOILING CAULDRON

THE THREAD WAS THEN WOVEN INTO CLOTH ON LOOMS IN THE HOUSES. FINALLY, THE CLOTH WAS WAULKED (BEATEN) TO SHRINK THE MATERIAL.

WOMEN GATHERED ROUND A TABLE AND SANG RHYTHMIC SONGS AS THEY WAULKED THE CLOTH.

125

WORK FOR THE ESTATE OWNER

YOU MIGHT NOT LIKE
YOUR LANDLORD
BUT YOU COULD WORK
FOR HIM AS A
SERVANT IN HIS HOUSE,
OR AS A GAMEKEEPER
OR GHILLIE (SERVANT)
ON HIS ESTATE.

DURING THE POTATO FAMINE
THE GOVERNMENT TRIED TO KEEP
STARVATION AT BAY BY
SENDING FOOD TO THE
HIGHLANDS. AT LEAST THE
NEW STEAM-POWERED
SHIPS COULD GET PLACES
QUICKLY WITHOUT HAVING TO
WAIT FOR A GOOD WIND.
REGULAR FERRY SERVICES
CREATED LINKS BETWEEN
MAINLAND AND ISLANDS. TWO
CANALS WERE BUILT TO CUT OUT LONG
SEA JOURNEYS. THE CALEDONIAN CANAL
LINKED EAST AND WEST COASTS. THE
CRINAN CANAL SAVED A LONG VOYAGE
ROUND THE MULL OF KINTYRE.

CALEDONIAN CANAL

CRINAN CANAL

CLYDE PUFFERS
BECAME FAMILIAR
SIGHTS IN THE HIGHLANDS
AND ISLANDS - CARRYING
COAL AND GENERAL
CARGO.

By now, the crofters had had enough. Rebellion was stirring in the glens and on the islands. Some tenants on the island of Skye demanded more land so they could keep their animals on it. Nobody listened. In protest, they refused to pay their rent. Suddenly, somebody listened. In Inverness, Sheriff Ivory exploded.

The Sheriff Officer was sent to Skye with notices of eviction. The crofters set fire to them. Sheriff Ivory exploded again.

50 policemen from Glasgow arrived on Skye. (Sheriff Ivory directed operations from a carriage at a safe distance.) There were scuffles and some Skye men were arrested. There were reporters there too, and the event made the headlines.

The Daily Gossip   *1882*

The Battle of The Braes!

Crofters make it clear they want change.

The arrested men appeared in court at Inverness. They were charged but got off with a small fine. They returned home as heroes. The government was very embarrassed.

But the trouble didn't stop. The crofters continued protest. Now, the military was called in. A gunboat appeared among the islands with a detachment of marines to back up the police.

Still the crofters complained. Eventually, the government sent some very important people with notepads. They travelled the length and breadth of the Highlands and Islands, looking at things and listening to complaints.

...ome muttering in parliament, the government
...d an Act.

CROFTERS'ACT

1. SECURITY: LANDLORD CAN'T THROW YOU
                 OUT OF YOUR CROFT.
2. COMPENSATION: IF YOU DO UP YOUR CROFT YOU
                 WILL BE PAID FOR THE IMPROVEMENTS
                 IF YOU LEAVE.
3. FAMILY: YOU CAN LEAVE THE CROFT TO
                 THE KIDS.
4. FAIRNESS: YOU CAN COMPLAIN IF YOU THINK
                 THE RENT IS UNFAIR.

But the crofters were farmers, and what they really
wanted was more land. They kept up their protests.
Estate fences were pulled down, and the landlords'
sheep driven off. Crofters on Lewis invaded the
landowner's deer park.

Sheriff Ivory (him again) sent 750 police and 250 marines to the Isle of Tiree. A handful of protesting crofters were arrested. On Skye, the women saw off the soldiers. All this unrest became known as the Land Wars. By the end of the century, things weren't ideal for the crofters, but they were getting better.

OLD BLACKHOUSES GIVEN CHIMNEYS AND GLASS WINDOWS

NEW STYLE HOUSES

In the next chapter: owner does the dirty by dropping dead, God worshipped on braes, boats and beaches, the glens are all trees and turbines.

CULTURE CARE

BY THE END OF THE 18TH CENTURY, SOME PEOPLE BEGAN TO THINK THAT HIGHLAND CUSTOMS AND CULTURE MIGHT DISAPPEAR.

The ban on Highland things after the Jacobite Rebellions has had a bad effect!

Let's form a Highland Society to promote Highland music.

AND BY THE END OF THE 19TH CENTURY, *AN COMUNN GAIDHEALACH* — THE HIGHLAND ASSOCIATION — HELD ITS FIRST *MOD* - A FESTIVAL OF MUSIC AND POETRY.

MAKING MUSIC

PIOBAIREACHD (PIBROCH) MEANS PIPE MUSIC. CEOL MOR (BIG MUSIC) IS THE CLASSICAL MUSIC OF BAGPIPES, USUALLY PLAYED BY SOLO PIPERS. CEOL BEAG (SMALL MUSIC) - DANCES SUCH AS REELS, STRATHSPEYS, JIGS AND MARCHES ARE USUALLY PLAYED BY PIPE BANDS.

THE CLARSACH (HARP) OFTEN ACCOMPANIED SINGING.

THE FIDDLE - MUSIC TO DANCE TO.

THE PEOPLE OF THE WEST LOVED SINGING AND IF THERE WAS A TASK TO DO, THEN THERE WAS A SONG TO GO WITH IT. WOMEN SANG *LUNNEAGS* – SONGS TO KEEP BOREDOM AT BAY DURING DAILY TASKS – AT HARVEST OR GRINDING MEAL, FOR INSTANCE.

MEN WOULD SING *IORRAMS* – ROWING SONGS WHICH KEPT EVERYONE PULLING IN THE SAME RHYTHM.

PORT-A-BHEUL (MOUTH MUSIC) WAS SINGING TO ACCOMPANY DANCING WHEN THERE WERE NO MUSICAL INSTRUMENTS HANDY. THE WORDS WERE USUALLY NONSENSE – IT WAS THE RHYTHM THAT WAS IMPORTANT.

A FAVOURITE PASTIME WAS LISTENING TO STORIES. PEOPLE WOULD *CEILIDH* (GATHER) IN A HOUSE TO LISTEN TO TALES ABOUT STRANGE CREATURES AND MYTHOLOGICAL HEROES.

CATTLE KEEP THE HOUSE WARM

CHICKENS ROOSTING IN THE BEAMS

BOX BED DIVIDING LIVING SPACE FROM BYRE

HANDY COAT-HOOKS MADE FROM A TREE BRANCH

WOODEN VESSELS FOR MILK AND CHURNING BUTTER

KIST OR CHEST FOR KEEPING CLOTHES, DISHES OR OATMEAL

FINN McCOUL (OR FINGAL) AND THE FEINN (HIS GANG OF WARRIORS) GOT UP TO ALL SORTS OF DARING DEEDS.

THE SILKIES- SEALS WHICH COULD SHED THEIR SKINS AND TAKE ON HUMAN FORM. IF A SILKIE MARRIED A REAL HUMAN, THEIR KIDS HAD WEBBED FEET!

THE MOST FAMOUS AND DISTURBING OF ALL WERE THE KELPIES OR EACH UISGE (WATER HORSES). THESE CREATURES CAME OUT OF THE DARK DEPTHS OF LOCHS. THEY APPEARED AS BEAUTIFUL, DOCILE HORSES WHICH ENTICED PEOPLE TO JUMP ON THEIR BACKS. ONCE THERE, THE RIDERS STUCK FAST AND COULDN'T JUMP OFF WHEN THE HORSE PLUNGED BACK INTO THE WATERY DEPTHS TO DEVOUR THEIR PREY.

The Time of Bridges

FROM ABOUT 1900

By the twentieth century, the Highlands and Islands seemed less far away. They were still in the same place, of course, but it was now much easier to get to them on trains, cars and ferries.

RAILWAYS
++++++++

INVERNESS

KYLE OF LOCHALSH

ABERDEEN

MALLAIG

PERTH

OBAN

GLASGOW

EDINBURGH

Tenants and landowners didn't seem any closer, though. Crofters still wanted more land and landowners didn't want to give it to them.

Just after the First World War, a property came on the market. The islands were snapped up by Lord Leverhulme, a wealthy soap manufacturer. Lord Leverhulme had plans for Lewis.

FOR SALE

LEWIS
AND
HARRIS
OUTER
HEBRIDES

LEWI
HARRIS

A LOT OF BOG, VERY ANCIENT ROCK, STUNNING VIEWS, ONE CASTLE.

PLANS TO CREATE INDUSTRY AND WEALTH ON LEWIS

* BUY FISHING BOATS
* BUILD ICE FACTORY
* BUILD CANNING FACTORY
* BUY SPOTTER PLANE TO SEARCH FOR HERRING SHOALS
* BUY CHAIN OF SHOPS THROUGHOUT THE COUNTRY TO SELL FISH
* BUILD HOUSES, ROADS, RAILWAY ETC.

But what the Lewis people wanted was land. They told
Lord Leverhulme . . .

Lord Leverhulme said . . .

Neither side would give in. Leverhulme went off in a
huff to Harris. He gave some of his Lewis land to the
parish of Stornoway, but many people were now out of
work because Leverhulme's plans had been abandoned.

In Harris, Lord L. started again. He decided to redevelop the village of Obbe. Houses, kippering sheds, weaving mills, roads and lighthouses were built. He even had some small islands blown up to improve the harbour. The transformation was complete when the village name was changed to Leverburgh. Then Lord L. dropped dead. His estates were sold off and all his plans had come to nothing.

IN 1934, ON THE ISLAND OF SCARP, JUST OFF THE COAST OF HARRIS, A STRANGE EXPERIMENT TOOK PLACE. A GERMAN ROCKET SCIENTIST CALLED GERHARDT ZUCKER WANTED TO SHOW THAT MAIL AND MEDICINES COULD BE TRANSPORTED BY ROCKET TO REMOTE PLACES. HE LAUNCHED A ROCKET CONTAINING 30,000 LETTERS TOWARDS HARRIS, BUT THE ROCKET EXPLODED IN MID-FLIGHT.

AT THE SAME TIME AS LORD LEVERHULME WAS
STARTING HIS PLANS FOR LEWIS, A TERRIBLE TRAGEDY
OCCURRED. A SHIP CALLED THE *IOLAIRE* RAN ONTO ROCKS
AND SANK AT THE MOUTH OF STORNOWAY HARBOUR. SHE
WAS CARRYING 284 YOUNG SOLDIERS RETURNING FROM
THE FIRST WORLD WAR BATTLEFIELDS. 200 MEN WERE
DROWNED.

DURING THE SECOND WORLD WAR, ANOTHER SHIP RAN AGROUND
— ON ERISKAY. IT WAS FILLED WITH A STRANGE CARGO OF
BATHROOM FITTINGS, FUR COATS AND BICYCLES — PLUS
THOUSANDS OF CASES OF WHISKY. THE GOVERNMENT WAS KEEN
TO KEEP THE DETAILS OF THE SHIP SECRET BUT MUCH OF THE
WHISKY FOUND ITS WAY ONTO THE SHORE THEN INTO ISLANDERS'
HOUSES.

SIR COMPTON MACKENZIE, THE NOVELIST, WROTE A BOOK ABOUT
THE EVENT WHICH WAS EVENTUALLY MADE INTO A FILM
CALLED 'WHISKY GALORE'.

In the 1920s, the Forestry Commission was founded. It brought jobs to the Highlands but it also changed the look of the glens with plantations of prickly fir trees.

In the 1940s, the Hydro-Electric Board was created. The high rainfall in the Highlands and the narrow glens were just right for building hydro-electric dams.

THE CHANGING CHURCH

After the 1745 Rebellion, there were three main religions in the Highlands – Church of Scotland, Episcopalian and Catholic. The Protestant Church of Scotland was the official religion of the country and members of the others were sometimes persecuted. The Episcopalians had been keen supporters of the Jacobite rebellions and now often had to worship in secret, even burying their prayer-books in their gardens during the week.

In the middle of the 19th century, there was a wee spot of bother in the Church of Scotland. A squabble broke out over whose job it was to appoint new ministers.

It is the congregation which should choose new ministers!

No, it is me, the Landlord, who should choose new ministers!

144

Eventually, some congregations decided on strong action. They left the Church of Scotland and formed their own churches.

These new congregations weren't really supposed to use Church of Scotland churches, but some people barricaded themselves into the buildings and soldiers had to be called to get them out.

Then there were even more arguments, and another split which was called the Disruption. 400 ministers walked out of the Church of Scotland.

Many landlords refused to give land to the Free Church to build churches. Sometimes the only place these congregations could hold a service was on the beach, below the high-tide mark, as that ground didn't belong to anyone.

Eventually, the Free Church found money and land to build churches. In the Highlands, most people joined the Free Church. This left Church of Scotland churches a bit empty. In one parish, the congregation consisted of the minister's housekeeper, his servant, and one man (who came only when he was sober).

Then the Secession Church and the Relief Church decided to join together.

Then the United Presbyterian Church and the Free Church decided to join each other.

But some members of the Free Church weren't happy about this . . .

And so the splits continued . . .

TODAY THE CHURCHES ARE STILL SPLITTING APART AND LIKE ELSEWHERE, CONGREGATIONS ARE SHRINKING. ON HARRIS AND LEWIS MANY PEOPLE ARE STRICT SABBATARIANS — THAT IS, THEY SEE SUNDAY AS GOD'S DAY AND A DAY OF REST. SHOPS DO NOT OPEN AND EVEN DRIVING A CAR IS DISCOURAGED. WHEN THE ISLANDERS HEARD ABOUT PLANS TO RUN FERRIES TO AND FROM THE MAINLAND ON A SUNDAY — THERE WERE PROTESTS AND THE PLANS WERE SHELVED.

THREE very HIGHLAND THINGS

SHINTY

SHINTY OR CAMANACHD IS AN ANCIENT GAME A BIT LIKE HOCKEY. SAINT COLUMBA WAS SUPPOSED TO HAVE BEEN A KEEN SHINTY PLAYER AND THERE IS A GRAVESTONE ON IONA WHICH SHOWS A SHINTY STICK (CAMAN) AND BALL. THE WORD SHINTY COMES FROM GAELIC SINTEAG (TO LEAP).

THE GAME USED TO BE PLAYED IN THE LOWLANDS, TOO. IT WAS PLAYED IN THE STREETS BUT WAS OUTLAWED BECAUSE IT BECAME TOO DANGEROUS.
THE RULES WERE STANDARDISED IN THE LATE 19TH CENTURY. TODAY THE GAME IS PLAYED IN THE HIGHLANDS AND PLACES WITH A LARGE HIGHLAND POPULATION (GLASGOW) AND THERE ARE TROPHIES, LEAGUES AND REGULAR FIXTURES.

HIGHLAND GAMES

THE VIKINGS AND THE HAD ALWAYS ENJOYED WRESTLING, THROWING THE FIRST ORGANISED PLACE AROUND 1820. FOR VISITORS AND PUTTING THE CLACH NEART (STONE OF STRENGTH) OR TOSSING THE CABER WERE TWO POPULAR ACTIVITIES.

ANCIENT CELTIC PEOPLES GAMES OF STRENGTH — HEAVY WEIGHTS, ALSO RUNNING. HIGHLAND GAMES TOOK THEY WERE GREAT ENTERTAINMENT LOCALS ALIKE.

TODAY, WRESTLING, ATHLETICS, SHINTY, TUG-O-WAR, SOLO PIPING, PIPE BAND DISPLAYS AND DANCING ARE INCLUDED.

151

WHISKY

WHISKY GETS ITS NAME FROM GAELIC *UISGE BEATHA* (WATER OF LIFE).

Whisky has been made in the Highlands for centuries, maybe even for thousands of years. In the Middle Ages it was usually made by monks as it was used as a medicine. King James IV must have been fond of the occasional glass of whisky because it gets a mention in the Royal Records.

1494 : Sold to Friar John Corr, eight bolls of malt to make whisky.

1506 Paid to the local barber-surgeon, to make whisky for the King's pleasure...

By now, farmers throughout the Highlands were making their weekly batches of whisky.

In the 16th century, the government began to try to control the making of whisky and put a tax on it. People just continued as before, using their whisky stills in secret, out-of-the way places. One man made his whisky at the top of the burgh hall clock tower.

The whisky had to be hidden from the prying eyes of the gaugers or excisemen (government inspectors) – in cow-sheds or coffins, or under granny's skirts.

By the beginning of the 19th century, whisky-making had become big business, and commercial distilleries appeared throughout the Highlands and Islands.

By the 1950s, many army, navy and airforce bases were sprouting up. The military were not here to keep the Highlands under control, as in the past, but to defend the country from outside enemies.

By the 1960s, road traffic was increasing and many of the Highlands single-track roads had to be improved. The first car-ferries began to sail between the islands.

By the 1970s, causeways were linking islands and bridges were leaping over lochs and firths.

In the 1980s, the Scottish Crofters Union looked after the affairs of crofters. There were Gaelic programmes on TV, rock bands singing in Gaelic and children doing all their lessons in Gaelic in schools.

By the 1990s, crofters were buying their land from landlords. The population was dropping as people drifted off to find work in the cities though people from elsewhere were coming to find the quiet life and settling in the Highlands.

What would the Bigfeet family put on their postcard if they visited the Highlands today?

Dear Flatnose Family,
Big Forests (trees a bit boring) big Mountains, lots of bog. Travelling around quite slow (winding roads). Plenty of sea so we've been taking ferries. Very quiet, not many people around — the young ones want to head off for the bright city-lights and jobs. However, they can do university studies at home now thanks to modern technology. Bungalows have replaced traditional houses. No wolves or bears but lots of deer. Beavers will come back soon. Very peaceful — might move in here as many others have done. Yours Family Bigfeet.

Family Flatnose
14 Home Camp Avenue
The Knoll,
Riverburgh.

List of Dates

End of the Ice Age – around 10,000 BC
People arrive in Scotland – around 6,000 BC
People farming – around 4,000 BC
Bronze Age – from around 2,000 BC
Iron Age – from around 700 BC
Romans in Scotland – AD 80–380
Kings of Dalriada – from around 300
Christianity arrives – around 400
Vikings arrive – around 800
King Kenneth I of Scots – 843–859
Somerled of Argyll – born? – died 1165
King Malcolm IV of Scotland – 1153–1165
Angus Mor of Argyll – 1249–1294
Battle of Largs – 1263
Angus II of Argyll – 1294–1329
King Robert the Bruce – 1306–1329
Donald II of Argyll – 1380–1420
King Robert III of Scotland – 1390–1406
King James I of Scotland – 1406–1437
Duke of Albany – 1339–1420
John II, Lord of the Isles – 1449–1498
King James III of Scotland – 1460–1488
King James IV of Scotland – 1488–1513
King James V of Scotland – 1513–1542
Mary Queen of Scots – 1542–1567

King James IV (and I) – 1567–1625

Fife Adventurers – 1599

King Charles I – 1625–1649

National Covenant – 1638

Earl of Montrose – 1612–1650

Archibald Campbell, 8th Earl of Argyll – 1607–1661

King Charles II – 1649–1685

Archibald Campbell, 9th Earl of Argyll – 1629–1685

Argyll's Rising – 1685

King James II (VII of Scots) – 1685–1689

King William – 1689–1702 and Queen Mary – 1689–1694

Battle of Killiecrankie – 1689

Inverlochy Fort – Begun 1690

Earl of Breadalbane – 1635–1717

Earl of Stair – 1648–1707

Glencoe Massacre 1692

Queen Anne – 1702–1714

Act of Union – 1707

King George I – 1714–1727

James Charles Edward Stuart (wanted to be King James VIII) – 1688–1766

Battle of Sheriffmuir – 1715

General Wade, Commander-in-chief, Scotland – 1725–1738

Inverness Fort – begun 1727

Fort Augustus – begun 1729

Charles Edward Stuart (Bonnie Prince Charlie) – 1720–1788

Battle of Culloden – 1746

Fort George – completed 1767

Bonawe Iron Furnace – 1753–1870

Inveraray Castle – 1773

The Clearances – mostly first half of 19th century

Queen Victoria – 1837–1901

The Disruption – 1843

Crofters Act – 1886